Deployment Journal
for Parents

Memories and milestones while my child is deployed

Rachel Robertson

Elva Resa ✳ Saint Paul

To all whose child serves in the military

Thank you to those whose encouragement means so much:
Mom, Dad, David, Itzchel, Jane, Annie, Kathie, Carrie,
Christy Lyon, Karen Pavlicin, and of course,
Hanna and Abby.

For my mom and dad, who are simply amazing, and whose support
has made all the difference in the world. — Rachel

Deployment Journal for Parents:
Memories and milestones while my child is deployed
© 2008 Rachel Robertson
All rights reserved.

Design by Andermax Studios.
Every effort has been made to identify and obtain permission from
the copyright owners of quotations throughout this work.
If we have omitted anyone, please contact us at staff@elvaresa.com.

ISBN 13: 978-0-9657483-9-1

Printed in United States of America.

Elva Resa Publishing
Saint Paul, Minnesota
http://www.elvaresa.com

❧ Where to Find It ☙

💗 *my journaling* ☆

Thoughts of you 6

About this deployment 14

Saying goodbye 26

Deployment 34

Homecoming 144

💗 *ideas for me to try and things for me to remember* ☆

Letters and emails 55

Care packages 62

Communication 69

Reaching out 78

Stress management 86

Managing fear 97

Defining my role 106

Activities with kids or grandkids 114

Homecoming and reunion 145

💗 *keeping track* ☆

Communication 170

Accomplishments 176

Milestones and special events 180

A parent's love...

When I had my first child, I realized for the first time how big the love of a parent could be. I often thought of this as I watched my in-laws cope with the deployments of their son, my husband. My mother-in-law, Gail, wrote this about her experience:

> It was so hard seeing my son leave for deployment to Iraq. This was my child. All the nurturing, protecting, guidance, love, hopes, and dreams I had for him seemed to hang in a fearful heartbeat as we said our final goodbyes.
>
> "I love you, Son."
>
> "I love you, too, Mom."
>
> I hugged him and I could feel my emotions going out of control, but for his sake I used all the strength I could find to smile and say that I would be praying for his safe return and that I'm proud of him. We left it at that.
>
> To help ease my anxiety, I read every article in the newspaper that related to the war; CNN became my favorite channel. I found the more informed I became, the better I could handle the situation. I also found comfort in every yellow ribbon I saw, every bumper sticker that said "Support our Troops," and family prayer. And, I found satisfaction knowing my son was well trained and equipped for this mission and with every fiber of my being, I looked forward to his return.

Parents of military service members must live with such an intense mixture of emotions, from pride to fear, faith to sadness, all while finding courage for your child while your own heart is trembling.

I used a journal during my husband's deployments. It was not very organized or fancy, but it was a place I could keep all my thoughts. I could let out all my fear, anger, frustration and worry. Having a special place to do this allowed me to let go of many of my feelings and be strong and positive the rest of the day. I could be who I wanted to be, feel what I wanted to feel, and say what I wanted to say without worrying about anyone else. My journal was so important to me; I wanted to help you have the same experience. Your story is an important one to tell, and there is no one better to tell it.

With thoughts of hope,
Rachel Robertson

This is one of my favorite pictures of you.
I have faith we will make the best of this deployment!

✐ Thoughts of You ✐

When you were young I had so many dreams for you...

❧ Thoughts of You ❧

Some of my favorite memories of you are...

❧ Thoughts of You ❧

I always knew you would...

Thoughts of You

If I could tell you anything, I would say...

Thoughts of You

I have never been more proud of you than when...

❧ Thoughts of You ❧

I was worried about you when...

❧ Thoughts of You ❧

Others in our family are thinking of you too...

"Anyone can give up,
it's the easiest thing
in the world to do.
But to hold it together
when everyone else
would understand
if you fell apart,
that's true strength."

About this Deployment

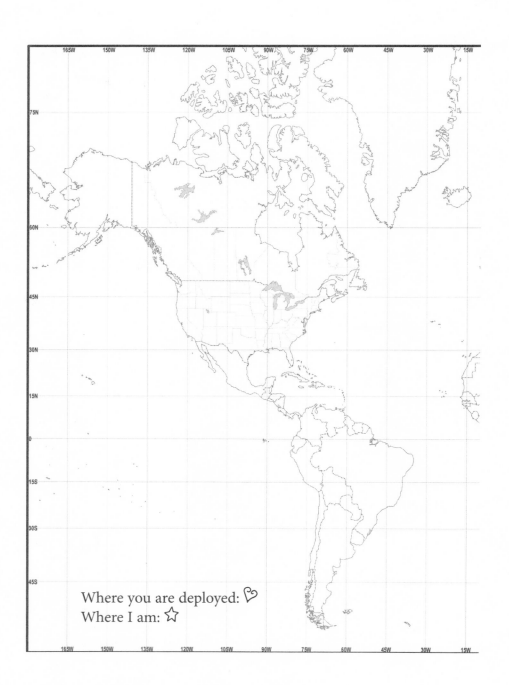

Where you are deployed: ♡
Where I am: ☆

Deployment Dates:

Deployment Location:

About this Deployment

How I heard the news...

❧ About this Deployment ❧

What I know about this deployment...

❧ About this Deployment ❧

What I want to know about this deployment...

"There is no friendship,
no love, like that of the
parent for the child."

~ Henry Ward Beecher ~

☆

❧ About this Deployment ❧

I am afraid of...

❧ About this Deployment ❧

I know there are many reasons why this deployment is happening...

About this Deployment

I know I may need support during this deployment.
Even though it's hard to ask for help I can count on these people...

Lord, grant me
the greatness of heart to see,
The difference in duty
and his love for me.
Give me the understanding to know,
That when duty calls he must go.
Give me a task to do each day,
To fill the time when he is away.
And Lord when duty is far away,
Please protect him, this I pray.
Amen.

I'm feeling...

.

strong, angry, hopeful, timid, proud, nervous, optimistic, furious, sure,

determined, exasperated, peaceful, worn out, useless, capable, empty,

frustrated, exhausted, faithful, mad, relieved, mean, loved, fed-up, overwhelmed, sad, terrified, excited, grateful, out of control, fulfilled, melancholy, joyous,

lost, blessed, spiteful, resentful, smart, heavy, fortunate, balanced

broken hearted, thrilled, lonely, playful, trapped, excited, reckless, peaceful, happy,

ᰄ Saying Goodbye ᰄ

We said goodbye on _____ (date)

What I want to remember about that day is...

∽ Saying Goodbye ∾

I didn't expect to feel...

Saying Goodbye

I wish...

❧ Saying Goodbye ❧

I hope...

"Promise me
you'll always remember
you're braver than you believe
and stronger than you seem
and smarter than you think."

❧ Pooh's Grand Adventure ❧

☙ Saying Goodbye ❧

I cried when...

❧ Saying Goodbye ❧

I was happy when...

Deployment

Now that you are gone, I feel...

I'm going to do these things to take care of myself...

∾ My Thoughts ∾

Today _____

"One day at a time~
this is enough.
Do not look back
and grieve over the past,
for it is gone;
and do not be troubled
about the future,
for it has not yet come.
Live in the present,
and make it so beautiful
it will be worth remembering."

⤞ Ida Scott Taylor ⤝

❧ My Thoughts ❧

Today _____

My Thoughts

Today _____

❧ My Thoughts ❧

Today _____

Find a Purpose
I don't simply have to endure deployment, I can make it work for me. I will find something
that gives each day purpose. A job. Volunteer work. Things I want to accomplish...

❧ My Thoughts ❧

Today _____

❧ My Thoughts ☙

Today _____

❧ My Thoughts ❧

Today _____

Today _____

Pride comes in many forms...

∽ My Thoughts ∾

Today _____

❧ My Thoughts ❧

Today _____

~ My Thoughts ~

Today _____

Tell me more... I wonder what it's like for you where you are deployed. .
Do you get any time alone? What do you do during the day? What do you do at night?
What do you do in your free time? What do you miss the most?

47

❧ My Thoughts ❧

Today _____

"Making the decision to have a child
— it's momentous.
It is to decide forever
to have your heart go walking around
outside your body."

❧ Elizabeth Stone ❧

🖤 🖤 🖤

Today _____

Is there a good kind of sadness? Is it caused by deeper love?

❧ My Thoughts ❧

Today _____

❧ My Thoughts ❧

Today _____

Today _____

Today _____

Letters and Emails
♡ ideas for me to try ☆

♡ Start a long letter and write in it every night for a week, sharing deeper thoughts than I normally would in an email.

☆ Send a letter (card, postcard, message in a bottle—whatever!) every other day or so. Letters don't have to be long, just a connection to home.

♡ Stock up on supplies. Set a letter-writing time each day.

☆ You are missing everything, so it's okay for me to write about the mundane.

♡ Share feelings and not just the facts about what's happening.

☆ Answer questions and be clear when asking questions.

♡ Keep a notebook somewhere and jot down things I want to remember to share in my next letter.

☆ Share current events or local news.

♡ Don't write to you when I'm angry or depressed. I can write out my feelings in a journal first and then write to you later when I feel better.

☆ Save our letters and emails in this journal or other special place as a keepsake.

♡ Keep track of important letters, emails, and phone calls on page 170 of this journal.

❧ My Thoughts ❧

Today _____

Today _____

Laughter feels so good.

❧ My Thoughts ❧

Today _____

❧ My Thoughts ❧

Today _____

❧ My Thoughts ❧

Today _____

Why is it we can still feel lonely in a room of people?

✎ My Thoughts ✎

Today _____

Care Packages
♡ tips for me to remember☆

♡ Send enough to share.

☆ Send favorites and some new things each time.

♡ Photocopy past and future calendar pages to share what our family has been up to and what is coming.

☆ Keep a box in the house and add to it each day, sending it at the end of the week.

♡ Encourage other members of our family to contribute or help with care packages. Grandma can be in charge of books and Uncle Joe can take care of hygiene products.

☆ Set a budget. It doesn't need to be expensive to be appreciated. I can be creative (ice packs for the desert!).

♡ Include a surprise in each package: a practical joke, homemade cookies…

☆ Include something that smells like home…

⤞ My Thoughts ⤝

Today _____

❧ My Thoughts ❧

Today _____

✎ My Thoughts ✎

Today _____

I wish I knew more about...

❧ My Thoughts ❧

Today _____

I loved it when you said...
I was upset when you said...

❧ My Thoughts ❧

Today _____

❧ My Thoughts ❧

Today _____

Communication

♡ tips and suggestions I'll keep in mind ☆

♡ Keep our communication positive.

☆ Appreciate the effort it takes to make a phone call.

♡ Make time in every communication to tell you I love you.

☆ Even though I'm eager to share, I'll remember to listen as well.

♡ I will try to see it from your perspective.

☆ I might not hear from you as much as I would like.

♡ I may not understand everything you are experiencing but I will be here whenever you want to share.

❧ My Thoughts ❧

Today _____

❧ My Thoughts ❧

Today _____

❧ My Thoughts ❧

Today _____

I wish you could have shared this moment with me...

❧ My Thoughts ❧

Today _____

❧ My Thoughts ❧

Today _____

~ My Thoughts ~

Today _____

Today _____

It's hard to be sad when you're dancing!

❧ My Thoughts ❧

Today _____

Reaching Out
♡ ways I can feel less alone ☆

Making new friends and helping others can be healing. There are many connections I can make:

☆ I can let my neighbors and coworkers know about my situation. People will support me if they know a little about what is going on in my life.

♡ I can join a support group in person or online with other military parents.

☆ I have something to offer others in need. I can support other military parents and families. I can help other people who have nothing to do with the military.

♡ I can adopt another service member or unit.

☆ Other places to make connections: local houses of worship, book clubs, family, USO, Red Cross, volunteering at local schools and hospitals, fitness centers.

My Thoughts

Today _____

❧ My Thoughts ❧

Today _____

Taking care of myself is so important...

❧ My Thoughts ❦

Today _____

❧ My Thoughts ❧

Today _____

❧ My Thoughts ❧

Today _____

∾ My Thoughts ∾

Today _____

I heard something on the news that made me nervous...

❧ My Thoughts ❧

Today _____

Stress Management
♥ ideas for me to try ☆

Even good changes in life cause stress. I can manage my stress. The important thing is to find something that works for me and to do it consistently.

♥ Exercise. Do yoga. Go for a walk.

☆ Pray or meditate.

♥ Play solitaire, do sudoku or crosswords, something to keep my brain busy.

☆ Listen to quiet music, or dance music.

♥ Cook or bake.

☆ Squeeze a stress ball or squishy toy.

♥ Take deep breaths.

☆ Count to ten before reacting.

♥ Leave notes around the house to myself: *You can do it!*

☆ Ask for help. Offer help. Learn to say no.

♥ Write a list of things I am thankful for.

☆ Drink lots of water.

♥ Eat well. Sleep.

☆ Start a new hobby. Read a good book.

♡ Punch a pillow.

☆ Keep a notebook by my bed to jot down thoughts that interrupt my sleep.

♡ Take a hot bath or hot shower.

☆ Limit TV or news watching to certain times in the day.

♡ Get takeout.

☆ Don't strive for perfection; strive for progress.

♡ Get a facial, massage, pedicure, or manicure.

☆ Remind myself this deployment is a temporary situation.

♡ Limit alcohol consumption.

☆ Smell something nice.

♡ Get a babysitter.

☆ Roam a bookstore. Sit by the ocean or in a park.

♡ Make time for myself every day.

☆ Cry. Laugh.

❧ My Thoughts ❧

Today _____

When I believe in myself, so do others.

~ My Thoughts ~

Today _____

❧ My Thoughts ❧

Today _____

❧ My Thoughts ❧

Today _____

❧ My Thoughts ❧

Today _____

You would have laughed when...

❧ My Thoughts ❧

Today _____

❧ My Thoughts ☙

Today _____

Worries

~ My Thoughts ~

Today _____

❧ My Thoughts ❧

Today _____

Managing Fear
♥ ideas for me to try ☆

Deployments cause untold amounts of fear and worry. There is sometimes no way to avoid fear, but there are things I can do to manage my fear.

♥ Write down my fears. Sometimes just getting them out diminishes them.

☆ Allow myself only one worry or sad time per week.

♥ Share my fears with a friend. Avoid being alone when I'm afraid or worried.

☆ Find out everything I can about the thing I'm afraid of. A lack of information contributes to fear.

♥ If I can't stop thinking about worst case scenarios, I will think them through and develop a plan for how I would deal with them. Sometimes just having a plan can calm my nerves and allow me to stop worrying.

☆ Buy or make a prayer box. Put my concerns inside and shut the lid.

♥ Let go of fears I have no control over.

☆ Talk to a professional if I think I might need it.

❧ My Thoughts ❧

Today _____

❧ My Thoughts ❧

Today _____

❧ My Thoughts ☙

Today _____

Hope brings us through.

❧ My Thoughts ❧

Today _____

❧ My Thoughts ❧

Today _____

Today _____

I can decide whether to merely survive or actually thrive. It's up to me.

❦ My Thoughts ❧

Today _____

❧ My Thoughts ❧

Today _____

Defining My Role
♥ things for me to keep in mind ☆

Parenting

♥ I can still parent you, even though you're grown and I might need to find different ways to do it.

☆ I can still show just as much concern as I did the first time you crossed the street by yourself. But I know that you are now an adult, in the armed forces, and you need my respect and to be treated with dignity.

♥ I will ask you what you need rather than assume. Sometimes taking care of your loved ones at home will be more important than caring directly for you. I understand that.

☆ I will try to communicate clearly and have the best of intentions.

Relating to other people who are important to you

♥ I will do my best to help your loved ones as well. This is a time to put any differences aside.

☆ I will communicate clearly about my hopes for our relationship and my role during the deployment.

♥ I will speak with kindness, ask what other loved ones need, and be consistent and reliable. Even though it might hurt, I will try not to be offended if they don't always accept or reciprocate.

☆ I know my role might change again after the deployment.

❧ My Thoughts ❧

Today _____

✎ My Thoughts ✎

Today _____

I especially missed you when...

⮂ My Thoughts ⮀

Today _____

❦ My Thoughts ❦

Today _____

My Thoughts

Today _____

❧ My Thoughts ❧

Today _____

What I wouldn't give for...

❧ My Thoughts ❧

Today _____

Activities with Kids or Grandkids
♥ ideas for me to try ☆

Deployments are hard on kids, too, but there are still lots of ways to make this time fun and memorable.

♥ Have family fun nights. Let children take turns selecting an activity.

☆ Take turns writing or telling a story together.

♥ Keep a family timeline during the deployment on a large piece of paper taped to the wall.

☆ Make a video during deployment. Plan, edit, and produce it just like a movie.

♥ Hold board game tournaments.

☆ Keep a scrapbook.

♥ Try to beat some of the records in the *Guinness Book of World Records.*

☆ Explore new places.

♥ Dance. Teach each other new dance moves.

☆ Have a sleepover in the living room.

♥ Leave love notes in their backpacks or under their pillows.

If I live far away...

☆ Send care packages to them, just like I send to you. They'll appreciate many of the same things: snacks, games, books.

♡ Write or tell them stories about when you were young.

☆ Read books over the phone.

♡ Send emails or play online games.

☆ Plan a weekly event that we'll each do simultaneously and then talk about afterward, like watch a favorite show or read the same chapter in a book.

♡ Collect something together, like coins or stamps, and trade them through the mail.

☆ Be consistent so they know they can count on me.

❧ My Thoughts ❧

Today _____

❦ My Thoughts ❧

Today _____

My Thoughts

Today _____

I am grateful for...

❧ My Thoughts ❧

Today _____

❧ My Thoughts ❧

Today _____

☆

"It's not only children who grow. Parents do, too.
As much as we want to see what our children
do with their lives, they are watching us
to see what we do with ours.
I can't tell my children to reach for the sun.
All I can do is reach for it myself."

❧ Joyce Maynard ❧

❧ My Thoughts ❧

Today _____

It's okay to feel stress, but it's not okay to let stress overwhelm me.

My Thoughts

Today _____

❧ My Thoughts ❧

Today _____

❧ My Thoughts ❧

Today _____

❧ My Thoughts ❧

Today _____

❧ My Thoughts ❧

Today _____

I thought of you when...

❧ My Thoughts ❧

Today _____

❧ My Thoughts ❧

Today _____

❧ My Thoughts ❧

Today _____

I wonder_

❧ My Thoughts ❧

Today _____

My Thoughts

Today _____

✎ My Thoughts ✎

Today _____

⟡ My Thoughts ⟡

Today _____

I want to remember to tell you about...

❧ My Thoughts ❧

Today _____

❧ My Thoughts ❧

Today _____

❧ My Thoughts ❧

Today _____

These memories make me smile...

❧ My Thoughts ❧

Today _____

❧ My Thoughts ❧

Today _____

❧ My Thoughts ❧

Today _____

My Thoughts

Today _____

❦ My Thoughts ❧

Today _____

"There's nothing
half so pleasant
as coming home again."

❧ Margaret Elizabeth Sangster ❧

❧ Homecoming ❧

You're coming home! This is how I found out...

Homecoming and Reunion
♡ things for me to remember ☆

♡ I will plan for a readjustment period. While you'll be happy to see us, you will also need time for yourself and to find your place in our lives again.

☆ I look forward to our reunion with excitement, but I will be prepared for the normal challenges that can come after a deployment. Deployment brings change and growth. No matter how much we hope that things will go back to the way they were before the deployment, I realize they probably will not, at least not right away.

♡ I will remember that we have each gone through a very meaningful—but very different—experience.

☆ I will be prepared to get reacquainted slowly and to understand that each person will adapt back to "normal life" in different ways.

♡ I will be there for you if you need someone to listen or to help as you adjust to being home again.

❧ Getting Ready for Homecoming ☙

I have to get ready. Before you come home I want to...

❧ Getting Ready for Homecoming ❧

I look forward to...
I hope...

❧ Getting Ready for Homecoming ❧

I wonder...

❧ Getting Ready for Homecoming ❧

I need you to understand...

❧ Getting Ready for Homecoming ❧

I am nervous about...

Getting Ready for Homecoming

I am planning to...

Getting Ready for Homecoming

I wish I had...

❧ Getting Ready for Homecoming ❧

I am so glad...

Homecoming

I want to remember the details of your homecoming.
Where... Time of day... Who was there... Your first words...

❧ Homecoming ❧

Things I want to remember about your first days home...

❧ Homecoming ❧

I am happy that...

Homecoming

I didn't expect...

❧ Homecoming ☙

I am grateful for...

❦ Homecoming ❧

Our other family members tell me...

⊱ Homecoming ⊰

This deployment...

~ Homecoming ~

This reunion...

❧ Looking Forward ❧

This experience is just one on our life's adventure.

~ Looking Forward ~

❧ My Thoughts ❧

Today _____

❧ My Thoughts ❧

Today _____

❧ My Thoughts ❧

Today _____

❦ My Thoughts ❧

Today _____

❧ My Thoughts ❧

Today _____

❧ My Thoughts ❧

Today _____

✎ Keeping Track ✎

Communication

Record of special moments when we've connected during this deployment, like the first call or a time I really needed to hear from you.

Date   Connection

_____   _____

_____   _____

_____   _____

_____   _____

_____   _____

_____   _____

Date   Connection

❧ Keeping Track ❧

Date   Connection

_____   _____
                _____
                _____

_____   _____
                _____
                _____

_____   _____
                _____
                _____

_____   _____
                _____
                _____

_____   _____
                _____
                _____

_____   _____
                _____
                _____

_____   _____
                _____
                _____

❧ Keeping Track ❧

Date   Connection

—————   —————————————————————————————————
            —————————————————————————————————
            —————————————————————————————————

—————   —————————————————————————————————
            —————————————————————————————————
            —————————————————————————————————

—————   —————————————————————————————————
            —————————————————————————————————
            —————————————————————————————————

—————   —————————————————————————————————
            —————————————————————————————————
            —————————————————————————————————

—————   —————————————————————————————————
            —————————————————————————————————
            —————————————————————————————————

—————   —————————————————————————————————
            —————————————————————————————————
            —————————————————————————————————

—————   —————————————————————————————————
            —————————————————————————————————
            —————————————————————————————————

❧ Keeping Track ❧

Date   Connection

_____   _____
              _____
              _____

_____   _____
              _____
              _____

_____   _____
              _____
              _____

_____   _____
              _____
              _____

_____   _____
              _____
              _____

_____   _____
              _____
              _____

_____   _____
              _____
              _____

✤ Keeping Track ✤

Date   Connection

_____   _____

              _____

              _____

_____   _____

              _____

              _____

_____   _____

              _____

              _____

_____   _____

              _____

              _____

_____   _____

              _____

              _____

_____   _____

              _____

              _____

_____   _____

              _____

              _____

❧ Keeping Track ❧

Accomplishments

I wasn't sure I could do it, but I did!

Date	Accomplishment
_____	_____
	_____
	_____
	_____
_____	_____
	_____
	_____
	_____
_____	_____
	_____
	_____
	_____
_____	_____
	_____
	_____
	_____
_____	_____
	_____
	_____
	_____
_____	_____
	_____
	_____

❧ Keeping Track ❧

Date   Accomplishment

_____   _____
              _____
              _____

_____   _____
              _____
              _____

_____   _____
              _____
              _____

_____   _____
              _____
              _____

_____   _____
              _____
              _____

_____   _____
              _____
              _____

_____   _____
              _____
              _____

⤝ Keeping Track ⤞

Date	Accomplishment
_____	_____
	_____
	_____
_____	_____
	_____
	_____
_____	_____
	_____
	_____
_____	_____
	_____
	_____
_____	_____
	_____
	_____
_____	_____
	_____
	_____
_____	_____
	_____
	_____

❧ Keeping Track ❧

Date   Accomplishment

_____   _____

              _____

              _____

_____   _____

              _____

              _____

_____   _____

              _____

              _____

_____   _____

              _____

              _____

_____   _____

              _____

              _____

_____   _____

              _____

              _____

_____   _____

              _____

              _____

Milestones & Special Events

So much has happened during this time...

Date   Milestones, special events, and other things to remember

_____   _____
                       _____
                       _____

_____   _____
                       _____
                       _____

_____   _____
                       _____
                       _____

_____   _____
                       _____
                       _____

_____   _____
                       _____
                       _____

_____   _____
                       _____
                       _____

❧ Keeping Track ❧

Date	Milestones, special events, and other things to remember
____	_____
	_____
	_____
____	_____
	_____
	_____
____	_____
	_____
	_____
____	_____
	_____
	_____
____	_____
	_____
	_____
____	_____
	_____
	_____
____	_____
	_____
	_____

❧ Keeping Track ❧

Date	Milestones, special events, and other things to remember

_____   _____

❧ Keeping Track ❧

Date   Milestones, special events, and other things to remember

_____   _____
                _____
                _____

_____   _____
                _____
                _____

_____   _____
                _____
                _____

_____   _____
                _____
                _____

_____   _____
                _____
                _____

_____   _____
                _____
                _____

_____   _____
                _____
                _____

❧ Keeping Track ❧

Date   Milestones, special events, and other things to remember

_____   _____

            _____

            _____

_____   _____

            _____

            _____

_____   _____

            _____

            _____

_____   _____

            _____

            _____

_____   _____

            _____

            _____

_____   _____

            _____

            _____

_____   _____

            _____

            _____

❧ Keeping Track ❧

Date	Milestones, special events, and other things to remember
————	_____
	_____
	_____
————	_____
	_____
	_____
————	_____
	_____
	_____
————	_____
	_____
	_____
————	_____
	_____
	_____
————	_____
	_____
	_____
————	_____
	_____
	_____

❧ Keeping Track ❧

Date   Milestones, special events, and other things to remember

_____   _____
                _____
                _____

_____   _____
                _____
                _____

_____   _____
                _____
                _____

_____   _____
                _____
                _____

_____   _____
                _____
                _____

_____   _____
                _____
                _____

_____   _____
                _____
                _____

ᴥ Keeping Track ᴥ

Date   Milestones, special events, and other things to remember

∽ Keeping Track ∾

Date   Milestones, special events, and other things to remember

_____   _____
            _____
            _____

_____   _____
            _____
            _____

_____   _____
            _____
            _____

_____   _____
            _____
            _____

_____   _____
            _____
            _____

_____   _____
            _____
            _____

_____   _____
            _____
            _____

❧ Keeping Track ❧

Date   Milestones, special events, and other things to remember

_____

_____

_____

_____

_____

_____

_____

∾ Keeping Track ∾

Date   Milestones, special events, and other things to remember

_____   _____
                _____
                _____

_____   _____
                _____
                _____

_____   _____
                _____
                _____

_____   _____
                _____
                _____

_____   _____
                _____
                _____

_____   _____
                _____
                _____

_____   _____
                _____
                _____

1G EUREKA!

Success in Science

Carol Chapman
Rob Musker
Daniel Nicholson
Moira Sheehan

Heinemann

Heinemann Educational Publishers
Halley Court, Jordan Hill, Oxford, OX2 8EJ
a division of Reed Educational & Professional Publishing Ltd
Heinemann is a registered trademark of Reed Educational & Professional Publishing Ltd

OXFORD MELBOURNE AUCKLAND
JOHANNESBURG BLANTYRE GABORONE
IBADAN PORTSMOUTH NH (USA) CHICAGO

© Carol Chapman, Rob Musker, Daniel Nicholson, Moira Sheehan, 2000

First published 2000

ISBN 0 435 57608 9

04 03 02 01 00
10 9 8 7 6 5 4 3 2 1

Edited by Ruth Holmes

Designed and typeset by Ken Vail Graphic Design, Cambridge

Original illustration © Heinemann Educational Publishers 2000

Illustrated by Barry Atkinson, Graham-Cameron Illustration (Tim Archbold, Darin
Mount and Sarah Wimperis), Nick Hawken, B.L. Kearley Ltd. (Sheila Galbreath,
Jeremy Gower and Pat Tourett), David Lock, Joseph McEwan, John Plumb, Sylvie
Poggio Artists Agency (Rhiannon Powell and Sean Victory), Linda Rogers Associates
(Lorna Barnard, Keith Howard, Gary Rees and Branwen Thomas)

Printed and bound in Spain by Edelvives

Picture research by Jennifer Johnson

Acknowledgments
The authors and publishers would like to thank the following for permission to use
copyright material: **bar chart p10**, Addison-Wesley, *Body Maintenance*; **graph p47**,
The Canadian Journal of Rural Medicine Vol. 3, p12–19, with permission from the Society
of Rural Physicians of Canada; **map p90**, Ordnance Survey Mapping with the
permission of the Controller of Her Majesty's Stationery Office, © Crown copyright,
Licence no. 398020.

The publishers have made every effort to trace the copyright holders, but if they have
inadvertently overlooked any, they will be pleased to make the necessary
arrangements at the first opportunity.

For photograph acknowledgements, please see page 152.

Everyone can

Understand science by

Reading this book, be

Enthralled, become

Knowledgeable and

Achieve success…

…with EUREKA!

iii

Welcome to *Eureka! Success in Science*

This is the first of three books designed to help you learn all the science ideas you need during Key Stage 3. We hope you'll enjoy the books as well as learning a lot from them.

These two pages will help you get the most out of the book so it's worth spending a couple of minutes reading them!

This book has nine units which each cover a different topic. The units have three types of pages:

Setting the scene

Each unit starts with a double-page spread which reminds you of what you know already about the topic. They tell you other interesting things, such as the place of science in everyday life and the history of some science inventions and ideas.

Learn about

► Energy

Most of the double-page spreads in a unit introduce and explain new ideas about the topic. They start with a list of these so that you can see what you are going to learn about.

Think about

► Fair tests

► Variables

Each unit has a double-page spread called Think about. You will work in pairs or small groups and discuss your answers to the questions. These pages will help you understand how scientists work and how ideas about science develop.

On the pages there are these symbols:

ⓐ Make a list of foods that give you a lot of energy.

Quick questions scattered through the pages help you check your knowledge and understanding of the ideas as you go along.

Questions

The questions at the end of the spread help you check you understand all the important ideas.

For your notes

These list the important ideas from the spread to help you learn, write notes and revise.

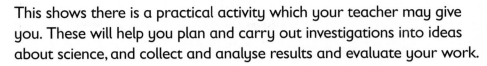

 This shows there is a practical activity which your teacher may give you. These will help you plan and carry out investigations into ideas about science, and collect and analyse results and evaluate your work.

 This shows there is an ICT activity which your teacher may give you. You will use computers to collect results from datalogging experiments, or work with spreadsheets and databases, or get useful information from CD-ROMS or the Internet.

 This shows there is a writing activity which your teacher may give you to help you write about the science you learn.

 This shows there is a discussion activity which your teacher may give you. You will share your ideas about science with others in a discussion.

At the back of the book:

 All the important scientific words in the text appear in **bold** type. They are listed with their meanings in the Glossary at the back of the book. Look there to remind yourself what they mean.

 There is an Index at the very back of the book, where you can find out which pages cover a particular topic.

Activities to check your learning

Your teacher may give you these activities:

Lift-off! When you start a unit, this short exercise reminds you what you already know about a topic.

Unit map You can use this to think about what you already know about a topic. You can also use it to revise a topic before a test or exam.

Quiz You can use the quiz at the end of each unit to see what you are good at and what you might need to revise.

Revision 1 You can use the revision sheets to revise a part of a unit which you aren't so good at.

End of unit test This helps you and your teacher check what you learned during the unit, and measures your progress and success.

Contents

Introduction iv

1 Energy
1.1 What does energy mean to you? 2
1.2 What is energy? 4
1.3 Energy on the move 6
1.4 Stored energy 8
1.5 Fuel for life 10
1.6 Sound energy 12
1.7 More energy, more sound? 14
1.8 Energy trails 16
T **1.9** The best fuel? 18

2 Changing state
2.1 The birthday party 20
2.2 Solids, liquids and gases 22
2.3 Particle power 24
2.4 Moving particles 26
2.5 Dissolving 28
2.6 Separating mixtures 30
T **2.7** Crime and colours 32

3 Living things
3.1 Lookalikes 34
3.2 Sorting out living things 36
3.3 More animal groups 38
3.4 Make no bones about it 40
3.5 Differences count 42
3.6 Born to survive 44
T **3.7** The right size? 46

4 Burning
4.1 The burning question 48
4.2 How does it happen? 50
4.3 Burning changes 52
4.4 Useful burning 54
4.5 What's special about fuels? . . 56
4.6 It's all about reactions 58
T **4.7** Getting hotter 60

5 Electricity
5.1 At the touch of a switch 62
5.2 Circuit training 64
5.3 Current affairs 66
5.4 Energy from electricity 68
T **5.5** Models of electricity 70
5.6 More circuits 72
5.7 Magnets 74
5.8 Electromagnets 76

6 Plant power
6.1 The history of microscopes . . 78
6.2 Building blocks 80
6.3 Photosynthesis 82
6.4 Leaf structure 84
6.5 The root of the problem 86
6.6 Plant reproduction 88
T **6.7** Scaling up and down 90

7 Metals

7.1 Metals through the ages. 92

7.2 What is a metal?. 94

7.3 Metals as elements 96

7.4 Non-metals 98

T **7.5** Getting it right 100

7.6 Heating metals 102

7.7 Rusting. 104

7.8 Compounds. 106

8 Forces

8.1 Sports day. 108

8.2 Forces and gravity 110

8.3 Friction 112

8.4 Unbalanced forces 114

8.5 Balanced forces. 116

8.6 Speed 118

T **8.7** Forces and relationships. . . . 120

9 Life story

9.1 A day at the zoo. 122

9.2 Spot the difference 124

9.3 A new generation 126

9.4 Pregnancy 128

9.5 Adolescence 130

T **9.6** Pregnant pause 132

Glossary 134

Index 144

> T indicates Think about spread

What does energy mean to you?

What is energy?

Energy has something to do with food.

a Make a list of foods that give you a lot of energy.

Energy has something to do with fuels.

b Make a list of as many fuels as you can think of.

Athletes need a lot of energy to run a long way. The further they run, the more food they need.

Moving has something to do with energy.

c Describe how you feel after you have run a long way.

Lifting weights makes you tired and hungry. Lifting things up has something to do with energy.

d Filling shelves at a supermarket involves a lot of lifting. Think of other jobs with a lot of lifting.

Things that give out light give out energy.

f Think of five things that give out light.

When something is hot, it is giving out energy.

e Make a list of things that feel warm when you touch them.

We have to pay for electricity. Electricity brings energy to our homes to make things work.

g Think about a room in your home. What things in the room work when you plug them in?

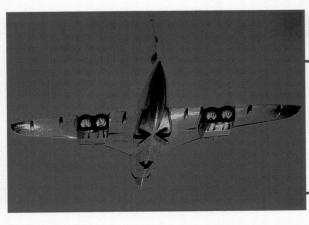

When a jet plane goes very fast, it makes a very loud noise. When there is a loud sound, there is a lot of energy.

h Think about supporters at a football match. What do they do to make a lot of sound?

Questions

Look at the pictures opposite.

1. Which things give out light?
2. Which things make sounds?
3. Which things feel hot?
4. Which pictures show things moving?
5. Which things have to be plugged in to make them work?
6. Which things would give you energy if you ate them?
7. Which pictures show things being lifted up?

What is energy?

Energy in action

That boy has lots of energy.

Eat your breakfast. It will give you energy.

You were very energetic today.

I haven't the energy to do that!

In science, we use the word 'energy' in a special way.

If something is moving, it has energy. We call this **movement energy**.

a How do you know that the skater has energy?

If something gives out light, it is giving out energy. We call this **light energy**.

b How do you know that the Sun is giving out energy?

If something makes sound, it is giving out energy. We call this **sound energy**.

c How do you know that the hi-fi is giving out energy?

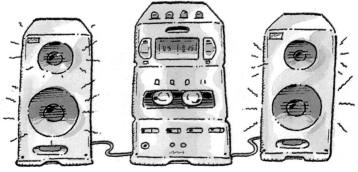

If something feels warm, it is giving out energy.
We call this **heat energy**.

d How do you know that the iron is giving out energy?

If something is happening, then **energy** is involved.

e Look at the photo. Imagine you are there. What would you see and hear and feel? What would be moving?

f Describe what is happening in the photo. Use the words 'light energy', 'sound energy', 'heat energy' and 'movement energy' as often as you can.

Questions

1. How can you tell that:

   a a TV is working?

   b a kettle is working?

   c a clock is working?

2. Copy and complete these sentences.

   We know a spinning top has energy because ...

   We know that a bell gives out energy because ...

   We know that a fire gives out energy because ...

3. Imagine you lived in the past, perhaps in a Stone Age village. What things would:

   a give out sound energy?

   b give out light energy?

   c show they have movement energy?

   d give out heat energy?

For your notes

Things that move have **movement energy**.

Energy given out as light is called **light energy**.

Energy given out as sound is called **sound energy**.

Energy that warms is called **heat energy**.

5

Energy on the move

Transferring energy

Energy moves from place to place. We say that energy is **transferred**.

Energy is transferred from a light bulb to our eyes. Energy is transferred from a radio to our ears. Energy is transferred from a heater to our skin.

a These things can be used to detect energy:

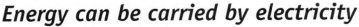

> **microphone   camera film**
> **thermometer   eyes   ears   skin**

Which two detect ('see') light energy?

Which two detect ('hear') sound energy?

Which two detect ('feel') heat energy?

Energy can be carried by electricity

When we switch on a lamp, the electricity transfers the energy to the lamp. The energy leaves the lamp as light energy.

When we switch on a radio, the electricity transfers the energy to the radio. The energy leaves the radio as sound energy.

When we switch on a heater, the electricity transfers the energy to the heater. The energy leaves the heater as heat energy.

We call energy transferred by electricity **electrical energy**.

b Look at the pictures opposite. You plug these things in to make them work. Electrical energy goes into each. What types of energy come out of each one?

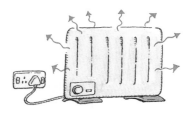

iron

radio

drill

cooker

Showing energy transfers

Energy transfers can be drawn using arrows. The arrows show which way the energy goes. Look at the energy transfers here for an electric heater and an electric radio.

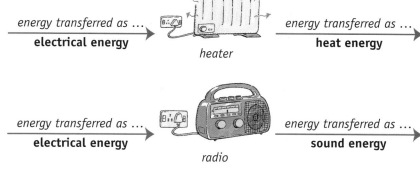

energy transferred as ...
electrical energy

heater

energy transferred as ...
heat energy

energy transferred as ...
electrical energy

radio

energy transferred as ...
sound energy

c Copy and complete this energy transfer diagram for an electric cooker.

energy transferred as ...
_____ **energy**

cooker

energy transferred as ...
_____ **energy**

An electric lamp gives out light energy as well as heat energy. The energy transfer diagram for a lamp has more arrows.

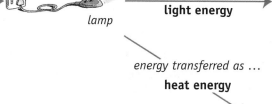

energy transferred as ...
electrical energy

lamp

energy transferred as ...
light energy

energy transferred as ...
heat energy

Questions

A hairdryer is plugged in to make it work. The hairdryer blows hot air and makes a lot of sound.

1. Copy and complete these sentences.

Energy is carried into the hairdryer by _____. We call this _____ energy. The hairdryer gives out air, which has _____ energy and _____ energy. The hairdryer also gives out _____ energy.

2. Draw an energy transfer diagram for the hairdryer.

3. Draw an energy transfer diagram for a TV.

For your notes

Energy can be moved from place to place. We say that the energy is **transferred**.

Energy transfers can be shown using energy transfer diagrams.

Energy carried by electricity is called **electrical energy**.

Stored energy

How is energy stored?

The arrow in the picture has movement energy. Where was the energy before it was moving the arrow?

The energy was stored in the stretched bow and bowstring. We call energy that is stored in something stretched **strain energy**.

a Think of three different things that can store energy as strain energy.

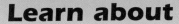

The bonfire is giving out light energy and heat energy. Where was the energy before it was light and heat energy?

The energy was stored in the wood. We call energy stored in materials **chemical energy**. Fuels, food and batteries all store energy as chemical energy.

The bucket and water have movement energy. Where was the energy before the water and the bucket started moving?

The energy was stored in the bucket and the water because they were lifted up. Things that are lifted up have energy because of gravity. We call energy stored because of gravity **gravitational energy**.

b How does a skier get energy so that she can go down the slope with lots of movement energy?

Energy can be **stored** in three ways. It can be stored as **strain energy**, as **chemical energy** and as **gravitational energy**.

In and out of storage

Look at the photos of the girl on the trampoline.

c Is the most energy stored in the trampoline at **A**, at **B** or at **C**?

d Is the energy stored in the trampoline as chemical energy, strain energy or gravitational energy?

e Is the most energy stored in the girl at **A**, at **B** or at **C**?

f Is the energy stored in the girl as chemical energy, strain energy or gravitational energy?

g When has the girl got most movement energy, at **A**, at **B** or at **C**?

We can show what is happening on the trampoline using an energy transfer diagram.

| *energy stored in the ...*
 trampoline
 as **strain energy** | → *energy transferred as ...*
 movement energy → | *energy stored in the ...*
 girl
 as **gravitational energy** | *energy transferred as ...*
 movement energy → |

Questions

1. How is the energy stored in **a**–**c**?
Choose from **gravitational energy**, **chemical energy** or **strain energy**.

   a a skydiver jumping out of a plane

   b a firework

   c a squashed ball

2. What energy is released from **a, b** and **c** above?

3. Draw an energy transfer diagram for each of **a, b** and **c**.

For your notes

Energy stored because a material is being pulled or pushed is called **strain energy**.

Energy stored in fuels, food or batteries is called **chemical energy**.

Energy stored in something because it is lifted up is called **gravitational energy**.

Fuel for life

Energy from food

Without food we would starve and die. Food is the fuel for our bodies. We call the energy stored in food **chemical energy**.

We get fat if we eat too much food and take too little exercise. We get thin if we eat too little food. The amount of energy we need from food depends on what we do.

The bar chart below shows you how much energy you need to do different tasks for one hour.

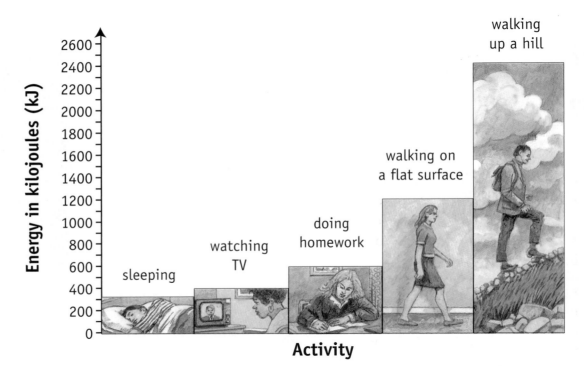

Energy in kilojoules (kJ) — Activity

sleeping, watching TV, doing homework, walking on a flat surface, walking up a hill

Energy is measured in **joules, J**. The bar chart uses **kilojoules, kJ**. One kilojoule is one thousand joules (1 kJ = 1000 J).

a How many kilojoules do we use to sleep for one hour?

The picture opposite shows how much energy is in some different foods.

b How much homework can you do using the energy in one slice of bread and butter?

sausage
500 kJ

fried egg
150 kJ

chips
1000 kJ

bread and butter
600 kJ

tea with milk
65 kJ

Telling how much energy is in food

Some foods are prepared for us, like frozen pizza. These foods come with a nutritional information label. This label tells us about the food. One of the things it tells us is the amount of energy in the food.

Nutritional information from a chicken and leek pie

Average values	per 100 g	per half pie
Energy	**1050 kJ**	**1975 kJ**

c Look at the food label above. How many kilojoules are there in half a chicken and leek pie?

d Sitting in a chair for an hour uses 395 kJ. How many hours can you sit in a chair using the energy in half a chicken and leek pie?

Foods like fruit, vegetables and fresh meat do not come with a nutritional information label. You have to look up the energy content of these foods in tables that you can get from your doctor, or buy in a bookshop.

Frank is on a diet. He wants to have a breakfast that uses 1500 kJ of his daily allowance.

e Make up a breakfast for Frank using the information in the table opposite.

Food	Energy per portion
Cornflakes	465 kJ
Milk (for cereal)	268 kJ
Milk (in tea or coffee)	65 kJ
Bread	352 kJ
Butter	297 kJ
Marmalade	166 kJ
Grapefruit	489 kJ

Questions

1. Use the information on these two pages to answer these questions.

   a Which contains more energy, a portion of butter or a portion of marmalade?

   b Which needs more energy, walking on the flat or walking up a slope?

   c How much energy would you take in if you ate a sausage and a portion of chips?

2. Why should you see your doctor before you start dieting to lose weight?

For your notes

Energy is stored in food as **chemical energy**.

Sound energy

How do we make sounds?

We make a sound when something **vibrates**. A vibration is made when something moves up and down, or from side to side. The steel drums vibrate.

How do we hear sounds?

We hear sounds with our ears. Look at the drawing of the ear. When a sound reaches our ears, the **eardrum** vibrates.

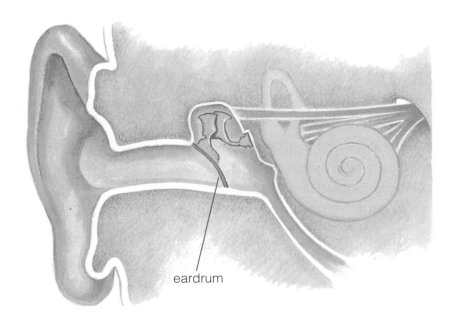

eardrum

ⓐ What happens to the eardrum when the sound reaches it?

When the **eardrum** vibrates, it makes some small bones vibrate.

The inner ear changes the vibrations into electrical signals. These electrical signals go down the **nerves** to the brain.

ⓑ How does the electrical signal get to your brain?

Your ear **transfers** the energy from the sound to your brain. Look at the diagram below.

energy transferred as … → **eardrum** and *small bones* → energy transferred as … → *inner ear* → energy transferred as …
sound energy   **movement energy**   **electrical energy** *along the nerve*

Getting to your ear

We know that sound is made by something that vibrates.
We know that we hear sounds using our ears. How does the sound get to our ears?

The table below shows what materials sound will travel through.

c Does sound travel through a vacuum?

Material	Will sound travel through it?
Air (Can we hear if there is only air around our ears?)	Yes
Water (Can we hear under the water?)	Yes
String (Can we hear using a string telephone?)	Yes
Wood (Can we hear sounds going through the table?)	Yes
Vacuum (Can we hear if there is nothing between us and the vibration?)	No

Sound needs a material to travel through. There is nothing in a vacuum, so there is nothing for the sound to travel through. Space is nothing, so sound cannot travel through space. This is one difference between light and sound. Light can travel through space, or it would not get from the Sun to Earth.

A L I E N

In space no one can hear you scream.

Questions

Jenny is listening to a band. The drummer plays a solo.

1. What part of the drum vibrates to make the sound?

2. How does the sound reach Jenny's ears?

3. What happens to Jenny's eardrum when the sound reaches it?

Imagine that the drummer is put in a sealed room and all the air is pumped out. (He would need to be in a spacesuit or he would explode!)

4. Would Jenny be able to hear the drums? Explain your answer.

For your notes

Sound is made by **vibrations**.

The **eardrum** vibrates when sound enters the ear.

Sound needs a material to travel though. It cannot travel through a vacuum.

More energy, more sound?

Making a sound louder

Big vibrations give loud sounds. Small vibrations give quiet sounds. We can see the vibrations on a **cathode ray oscilloscope** (**CRO** for short).

The **amplitude** tells us how big the vibrations are. The larger the amplitude, the louder the sound.

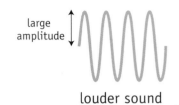

large amplitude

louder sound

small amplitude

quieter sound

Loud sounds have more energy

We measure the loudness of sounds in **decibels**, **dB**. A very quiet whisper might be 1 dB. A loud sound, like a vacuum cleaner, is 70 dB. A jet plane overhead is about 100 dB.

Loud sounds can hurt. Sounds of over 120 dB can damage the eardrum.

Quieter sounds do not damage the eardrum but they can still harm your hearing. Sounds of more than 90–100 dB can be dangerous if they go on for a long time. The sound damages the nerve that takes signals from your ear to your brain. People with noisy jobs have to wear ear protectors.

a The music in some clubs is played at about **110 dB**. People working in the club are at a high risk of damaging their hearing. Why?

Changing the pitch of a sound

The **pitch** of a sound is how high or low it is. Quick vibrations give high-pitched sounds. Slow vibrations give low-pitched sounds. Again, we can see the vibrations on a CRO.

The **frequency** tells how quick the vibrations are. The higher the frequency, the higher the pitch of the sound.

Frequency is measured in **hertz**, **Hz** or **kilohertz**, **kHz**. There are 1000 Hz in 1 kHz.

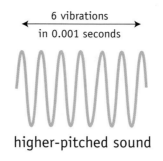

6 vibrations in 0.001 seconds

higher-pitched sound

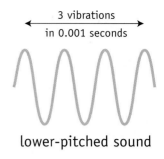

3 vibrations in 0.001 seconds

lower-pitched sound

Frequency in kilohertz (kHz)

0 — Some people can hear very low-pitched sounds of 20 Hz (0.02 kHz).
1
2
3
4
5
6 — The 'th' sound, like in 'thing', is a high-pitched sound of 6 kHz.
7
8
9
10
11
12 — Elephants hear up to only 12 kHz.
13
14
15 — Many older humans cannot hear high-pitched sounds above 15 kHz.
16
17
18
19
20 — Some humans (young ones!) can hear very high-pitched sounds, up to 20 kHz.

Dogs can hear up to 46 kHz.

Bats can hear up to 150 kHz.

Hearing the sound

Some people can hear more sounds than others. Different animals hear different frequencies. Look at the diagram at the side of the page.

b Who can hear sounds of higher frequency, young people or older people?

c Name two animals that can hear higher-frequency sounds than humans can.

Questions

1. Copy and complete these sentences.

The _____ of a vibration tells us how big the vibration is. Big vibrations make _____ sounds. The _____ of the vibration tells us how fast the vibration is. Fast vibrations make sound with a high _____.

2. Write out each sound below along with the correct number of decibels.

loud thunderclap   whispering   busy street   chatting

60 dB   30 dB   70 dB   110 dB

For your notes

Loud sounds can damage your hearing.

The larger the **amplitude** of a vibration, the louder the sound.

The larger the **frequency** of a vibration, the higher the **pitch** of the sound.

Some people can hear higher-pitched sounds than others.

15

Energy trails

Tracking the energy

Energy can be moved about. Energy can be stored. However, it is impossible to make or get rid of energy. We say that energy is **conserved**.

The people are talking about the energy in a banana. We can show this using an energy transfer diagram.

Sun — energy transferred as ... **light energy** → *energy stored in the ...* banana *as chemical energy*

a Bananas contain energy. Where did this energy come from?

Look at the picture above. Again, we can show an energy transfer diagram for the cloud.

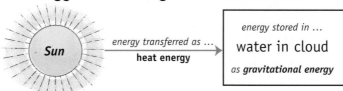

Sun — energy transferred as ... **heat energy** → *energy stored in ...* water in cloud *as gravitational energy*

b The rain has movement energy as it falls. Where did this energy come from?

An athlete lifts some weights. The weights now have gravitational energy. The energy transfer diagram below shows how the energy got from the Sun to the lifted weights.

c Copy the energy transfer diagram below, filling in the missing bits.

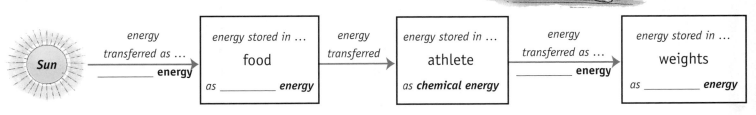

Not all the energy is useful to us

When the athlete lifts the weights he gets hot. Not all the energy is used to lift up the weights. Some is transferred as heat energy instead. We show this as a side arrow.

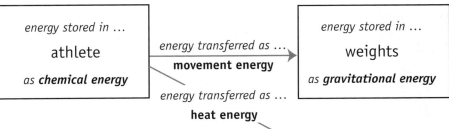

Think about a car. It has a store of chemical energy (the fuel). You want all the energy in the fuel to end up as movement energy. However, the engine gets hot and is noisy.

d Draw an energy transfer diagram for a car.

Questions

1. Energy is stored in:

  a a pat of butter (as chemical energy)

  b a jet plane up in the air (as gravitational energy)

  c a drawn bow (as strain energy).

Draw energy transfer diagrams to show how energy from the Sun ended up stored in each.

2. Think about a TV. You plug in a TV to make it work. You see and hear the TV. The TV also gets hot.

  a Draw an energy transfer diagram for the TV.

  b Which is the unwanted energy?

For your notes

Energy is **conserved**. It is impossible to create or destroy energy.

Most energy can be tracked back to the Sun.

When energy is transferred, only some of it can be used.

The best fuel?

Think about
► Fair tests
► Variables

Investigating fuels

A class investigated the energy given out by two different fuels, lighter fuel and firelighters. They burned the fuels and heated water with them.
The fuel that heated up the water more gave out more energy.
The class tested each fuel in turn.

a They decided to use the same mass of fuel each time.
Why do you think they did this?

b They decided to heat the same volume of water with each fuel.
Why do you think they did this?

The pictures below show Shaibal and Pippa's experiment with lighter fuel.

1. They used 100 cm³ of water and 2 g of fuel.

2. They took the temperature of the water at the start and found it was 21 °C.

3. They took the temperature when all the fuel had burned away and found that it was 46 °C.

4. They took the start temperature away from the end temperature to find out how much the fuel had heated the water:

$$\begin{array}{r} 46 \\ -\ 21 \\ \hline 25\,°C \end{array}$$

Each group then did another experiment using firelighters instead of lighter fuel. They wanted to compare the firelighters with the lighter fuel.

Shaibal and Pippa burned 5 g of firelighter and heated 100 cm³ of water. The temperature of the water was 21 °C at the start and 82 °C at the end.

c How much did the fuel heat the water?

d Did they use the mass of fuel the class had planned?

e Did they use the volume of water the class had planned?

f Do you think this was a fair test? Explain your answer.

g Would you have done the experiment in the same way as Shaibal and Pippa? Explain your answer.

Variables

There are three things that could be different at the start of this investigation:

- the type of fuel
- the mass of fuel
- the volume of water.

We are investigating types of fuel so this is the only one we change. It is called the **input variable**.

The change in water temperature depends on the type of fuel being used. This is called the **outcome variable**. This is the variable that we measure.

Shaibal and Pippa then did another investigation. They used lighter fuel for all their experiments. Their results are shown in the table below.

h What variable did they change? (This is the input variable.)

i What did they measure to get their results? (This is the outcome variable.)

j What variables did they keep the same to make it a fair test?

Mass of fuel in g	Amount of water in cm³	Temperature of water at start in °C	Temperature of water at end in °C	Temperature rise in °C
1.0	100	21	33	12
1.5	100	21	38	17
2.0	100	21	46	25

The birthday party

Cake and ice lollies

Sarah was helping with her little brother Matthew's birthday party. First she made chocolate icing for the birthday cake. She warmed pieces of chocolate in a bowl. The chocolate slowly become softer. Once the chocolate was nice and runny Dad poured it on top of the cake and left it to cool.

a What happened to the chocolate as it got hotter?

b What do you think will happen to the chocolate as it cools down?

As it was summer, Matthew and his friends were going to play outside. Mum said they would get hot. Sarah decided to make them some ice lollies. She poured some orange squash into a jug of water and stirred it to mix it well. Then she poured the mixture into the lolly moulds and put them into the freezer. She kept checking to see when they were ready. Gradually ice started to form on top. It took several hours before they were ready.

c What was happening when the lolly mixture was put in the freezer?

d What happens to an ice lolly when you suck it?

Balloons and bubbles

There was still plenty of time before the party. Sarah helped Mum with the decorations. She started by blowing up some balloons. Dad had bought Matthew a special one. It was filled with a very light gas and it floated up to the ceiling and stayed there.

'Blowing up balloons is thirsty work,' puffed Sarah. She poured them all a glass of lemonade. Sarah sat and watched the bubbles on the inside of her glass. Every now and then a bubble would float up to the top and vanish. 'I wonder why bubbles go up but not down,' she thought.

e Why did the special balloon float to the ceiling?

f Why do you think the bubbles went up but not down?

Ice cream and candles

Matthew's friends came and he had lots of presents. Everyone sang 'Happy Birthday' as Mum came in with the cake. Sarah could see how the tops of the candles were melting and the wax was running down.

They had ice cream and jelly. Dad got the ice cream out of the freezer. It was much too hard to get out of the tub. They had to leave it for a few minutes to soften.

g What was happening to the candle wax?

h Why did the ice cream have to be left out for a while?

Questions

1. Copy the table opposite and complete it by putting a tick in the correct column.

2. Copy and complete the sentences. Choose words from the word wall opposite to fill in the gaps.

   When you heat a solid, it can turn into a _____.
   This is called _____.
   If you boil a liquid, it will turn into a _____.
   Freezing happens when a _____ turns into a _____.

	Solid	Liquid	Gas
Chocolate in the fridge			
Water from the tap			
Ice cream from the freezer			
Air inside a balloon			
Hot wax running down a candle			

gas	solid	liquid	dissolving	solution

changing	melting	freezing	boiling

3. Write a story about a day out at the beach. Describe all the solids, liquids and gases that you find there.

Solids, liquids and gases

Different properties

Everything we can pick up or touch is made of **matter**. Solids, liquids and gases are three kinds of matter. They behave in very different ways. A solid is different from a liquid, and they are both very different from a gas. They have different **properties**.

Solids

The saucepan in the photo is an example of a **solid**. Solids are hard and they cannot be squashed easily.

If you put it somewhere else, this saucepan will still have the shape of a saucepan. The shape of a solid is the same wherever you put it. We say that it has a fixed shape.

This saucepan will have the same volume everywhere. The volume of a solid stays the same wherever you put it.

Solids are also very difficult to pour.

a Make a list of five things in the room around you that are solids.

b Write down two properties of solids.

Liquids

The drink in the photo is an example of a **liquid**.

Liquids are not hard like solids. They can be poured from one container to another. Some liquids, such as water, are very runny. They flow very quickly. Other liquids, such as oil, are much thicker. They flow much more slowly.

Like solids, liquids cannot be squashed. The diver in the cartoon below is about to find this out!

The drink in the photo has the same shape as the glass it is in. Before it came out of the bottle, the drink was bottle-shaped. The shape of a liquid is not fixed, it can change easily.

The volume of the liquid stays the same in any container. One litre of drink will fit into lots of different containers, but it will always be one litre.

c List four properties of liquids.

Gases

The air inside these balloons is an example of a **gas**.

Gases are not hard like solids. They can flow from one place to another like liquids do. The photo below shows how you can pour a gas.

The shape and volume of a gas does not stay the same. It changes to fill up all the container. The gas inside a balloon is balloon-shaped.

It is very easy to squash a balloon. All gases can be squashed easily.

d List four properties of gases.

Questions

1. Copy and complete these sentences.

Everything in the world is made of _____.
Solids, liquids and gases are three kinds of _____.

2. Copy the table. Complete it by putting either a tick (✔) or a cross (✗) in each box.

Property	Solid	Liquid	Gas
Easy to pour	✗	✔	✔
Easy to squash			
Fixed shape			
Fixed volume			

3. What properties do solids have that make them useful for building houses?

For your notes

Solids are hard and have a fixed shape and fixed volume.

Liquids have a fixed volume. They are runny and can be poured.

Gases do not have a fixed shape or a fixed volume. They take the shape of their container. They can be squashed easily.

Particle power

A closer look

You have already seen that solids, liquids and gases behave in different ways. Why is a solid hard? Why is a liquid runny? To find out, let's take a closer look at them.

Scientists think that everything is made of tiny **particles**. These particles are arranged in different ways in solids, liquids and gases.

Solids

In a solid, the particles are very close together. The particles are joined strongly. They are arranged very tightly in a neat pattern. They cannot move about, so the shape of the solid does not change.

Solids cannot be squashed because the particles are already very close. It is difficult to get them any closer because they are already touching.

a Describe how the particles are arranged in a solid.

Liquids

In a liquid, the particles are almost as close together as they are in a solid. They are close enough to make it difficult to squash the liquid.

In a liquid, the particles are not arranged in a neat pattern. They are not joined as strongly as the particles in a solid. They can slide over each other easily. This is why the shape of a liquid can change. You can pour and stir a liquid because the particles can move around easily.

b Describe how the particles are arranged in a liquid.

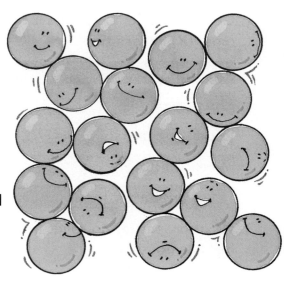

Gases

In a gas, the particles are very far apart. The gas can be squashed easily because there is space between the particles. They can be moved closer together. The particles in a gas are not joined to each other at all.

The particles in a gas move all over the place in a random way. Because they are always moving they will fill up their container. The shape and volume of the gas changes to match the container.

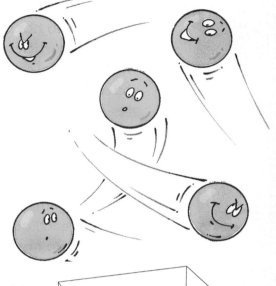

c Describe how the particles are arranged in a gas.

d Explain why the shape of a gas does not stay the same.

Density

The cube in this picture has lots of particles packed into a small volume. This makes it heavy. The cube is **dense**. Most solids are dense. Many liquids are also dense.

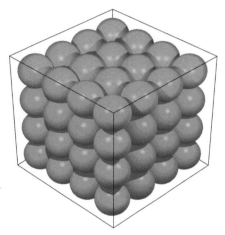

The cube in this picture has only a few particles in a small volume. This makes it lighter than the other cube. It is less dense. Gases are not very dense.

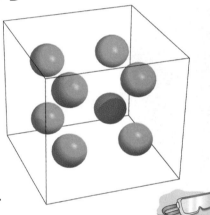

Questions

1. Copy and complete these sentences. Use words from the word wall to fill the gaps.

| joined strongly | not joined | not moving | move a little | moving | move a lot |

Solids have a fixed shape because their particles are _____.

Gases fill all of their container because their particles are always _____.

Liquids are easy to pour because their particles can _____.

2. Why are solids harder than gases?

3. a Which is heavier, 1 kg of water or 1 kg of steam?

b Which takes up the most space?

c Which is denser?

For your notes

Everything is made of **particles**.

In a solid, the particles are very close and in a neat pattern.

In a liquid, the particles are slightly further apart and have a less regular pattern.

In a gas, the particles are far apart and have no pattern at all.

Solids and liquids are more **dense** than gases.

Moving particles

How particles move

Particles do not stay still. They are always moving. Particles in solids, liquids and gases move in different ways. The more energy they have, the more they move.

Learn about

➤ Melting, evaporating and freezing

Melting and freezing

In a solid, the particles are joined together and very close to each other. The particles do not move about, but they jiggle from side to side. We say that they are **vibrating**.

a Describe how the particles in a solid move.

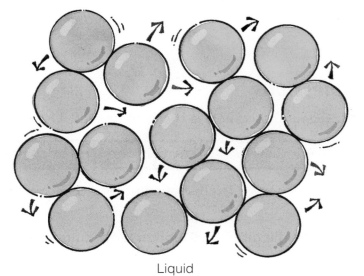

Solid

In a liquid, the particles are not lined up in rows, so they take up a bit more space. They are not joined very tightly. In a liquid, the particles are able to move about more than the particles in a solid.

b Describe how the particles in a liquid move.

Liquid

If you heat a solid, the particles start to jiggle faster. If they jiggle very fast, they move away from each other and are not joined so tightly. When this happens, the solid turns into a liquid. We say that the solid is **melting**.

The opposite of this is **freezing**. The particles slow down as they get colder. They get closer together and turn back into a solid.

Evaporating and condensing

In a gas, the particles are very far apart from each other. They are always moving around all over the place.

c Describe how the particles in a gas move.

When you heat a liquid, the particles move faster. They can move around so much that some of them break away from the other particles and move around on their own. Some of the liquid turns into a gas. We say the liquid is **evaporating**.

The opposite of this is **condensing**. The particles slow down as they lose heat energy. They get closer together and form a liquid.

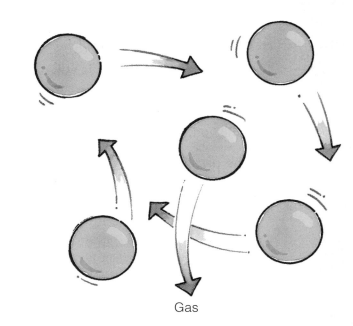

Gas

Changes of state

These changes from solid to liquid or liquid to gas and back again are called **changes of state**. Solids, liquids and gases are the **three states of matter**.

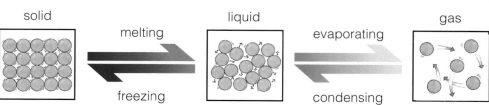

solid   liquid   gas

melting   evaporating

freezing   condensing

Questions

1. Copy and complete these sentences.

   When you heat particles, they move …

   When you cool particles, they move …

2. Imagine that you are a particle of water in an ice cube. Write a poem about what happens to you when you are put in a sunny place.

For your notes

Particles move faster when they are heated. They slow down when they are cooled.

A solid melts because the particles move away from each other.

A liquid evaporates because the particles move around on their own.

These changes are called **changes of state**.

Dissolving

Where does it go?

When you add sugar to a cup of tea, the sugar seems to disappear. You know it is still there because you can taste it. The sugar hasn't really vanished, it has **dissolved**.

The picture below shows what happens to the particles when sugar dissolves in water.

sugar
(solute)

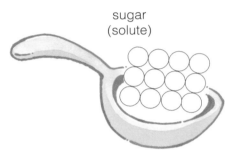

water
(solvent)

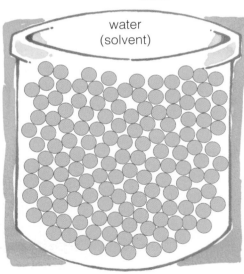

sugary water
(solution)

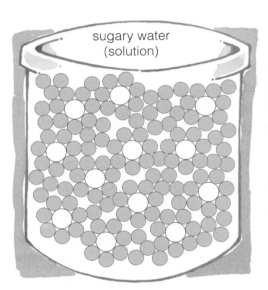

The particles in the sugar break apart and mix with the water particles. You cannot see the sugar particles because they are spread throughout the liquid. This is called a sugar **solution**.

The substance that dissolves is called the **solute**. The liquid that it dissolves in is called the **solvent**. The mixture of solute dissolved in solvent is called a **solution**.

a What is the solute in the example above?

b What is the solvent in the example above?

If you keep adding sugar, it will start to sink to the bottom rather than dissolving. No more sugar can dissolve. We say that the solution is **saturated**.

Speed it up

To make the sugar dissolve faster, you can do the following:

- Use hotter water. The particles move around more and so get mixed up faster.

- Stir it. The particles move around more, helping to mix up the sugar and the water.

- Use finer sugar. If you use a sugar cube, the particles on the outside will dissolve first. Particles in the middle of the cube will stay dry for quite a while. If you crush the cube up, then a lot more of the sugar is getting wet.

> **Did you know?**
> Sugar and salt will not dissolve in petrol.

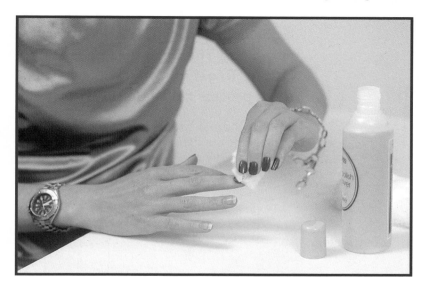

Different solvents

Some substances, such as nail varnish, do not dissolve in water. Nail varnish is **insoluble** in water. To remove nail varnish, you have to use a liquid called acetone. This is another type of solvent. The nail varnish will dissolve in the acetone – it is **soluble** in acetone.

Some felt-tip pens are filled with waterproof ink. You can use them to label test tubes. The ink is insoluble in water, so it does not dissolve when it gets wet. To remove the ink, you have to use alcohol.

Questions

1. Copy and complete the sentences below. Use words from the word wall to fill the gaps.

dissolve	solvent	solute
solution	soluble	insoluble

If you stir salt into water, it will _____.
The salt is called the _____ and the water is called the _____. The mixture of salt and water is called a _____.

2. Joanna put a sugar lump into a cup of cold water. It took a long time to dissolve. Give three ways of making the sugar dissolve quicker.

For your notes

A **solute** is a substance that **dissolves** in a liquid called a **solvent**. The particles in the solute break apart and mix with the particles in the solvent.

The mixture of solute dissolved in solvent is called a **solution**.

Different solutes dissolve in different solvents.

Separating mixtures

Getting drinking water

Imagine that you are on a desert island. There is no fresh water for you to drink. Sea water is not good to drink. It is a solution of salt in water. How could you separate the water and the salt to get drinking water?

If you boiled the water, it would turn into a gas. The salt would be left behind. To get drinking water, we can use a process called **distillation**.

3 The water vapour starts to travel down the condenser. This cools the vapour and it condenses back into liquid water.

condenser

2 The salt does not boil. It starts to form crystals at the bottom of the flask.

4 The water runs down the condenser and drips into the beaker.

5 This water is **pure**. It has no other substances in it. We call it **distilled water**.

1 The salty water is heated until it boils. When it boils, the water turns into a gas. We call this gas **water vapour**.

heat

ⓐ What happens to the water particles in the flask?

ⓑ What happens to the water particles in the condenser?

Pure water

Distilled water is **pure**. It has no other substances mixed in with it. If you boiled pure water, nothing would be left behind.

Separating inks

The ink in your pen is probably not made of one colour. It is a **mixture** of different colours or dyes. To separate them out, we can use a method called **chromatography**.

On wet paper, each colour will move differently. Colours that are very soluble move a long way. Colours that are not very soluble do not move very far.

Look at the picture below.

c Which one of these inks is a mixture?

d Which colour moved the furthest?

e Which colour moved the least?

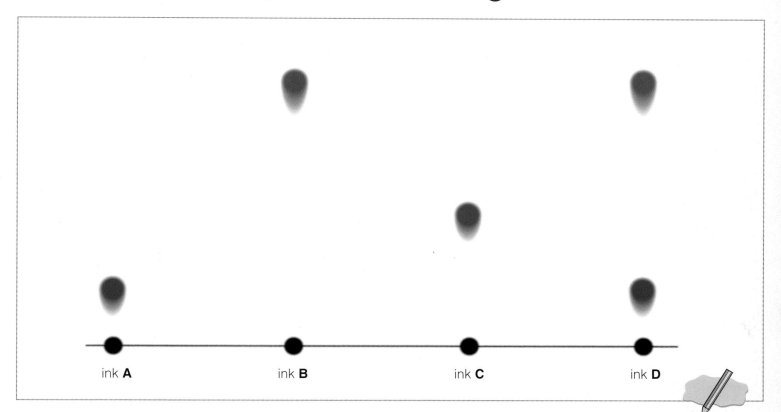

ink **A**   ink **B**   ink **C**   ink **D**

Questions

1. Copy and complete these sentences. Use words from the word wall to fill the gaps.

gas	vapour	distillation	distilled	condenses

To separate salt and water, we can use a method called
_____. The water is boiled and turns into a
_____. The water _____ reaches
the condenser where it cools down and
_____. This pure water is called
_____ water.

2. Is the ink in your pen a mixture? How could you find out?

For your notes

Distillation can be used to separate a pure liquid from a solution.

Chromatography is a way of separating a mixture of colours.

Think about

➤ Analysing results

Finding Mr X

Shaheen is a forensic scientist. She helps the police solve crimes. She analyses the results of her investigations carefully.

Mr Jones's garden gnome Bob has been kidnapped. A note from the kidnapper was signed 'Mr. X' in blue felt-tip pen.

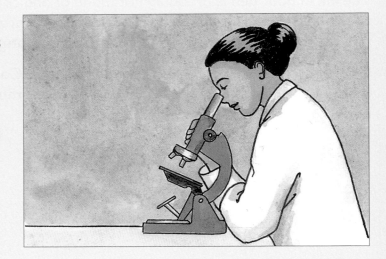

I have Bob the gnome, and I want £100

Mr X

Mr Jones thinks that one of his neighbours has kidnapped Bob. The police found a blue felt-tip pen in four of his neighbours' houses.

They need to prove that one of these pens was the one used to write the ransom note. Using chromatography, Shaheen separated the ink on the ransom note into its different colours. Her results are shown below.

ⓐ How many different colours do you think are in the blue ink?

ⓑ Which colour travelled the furthest?

Shaheen then did the same thing for each of the neighbours' pens. She compared these with the kidnapper's pen. Her results are shown on the next page.

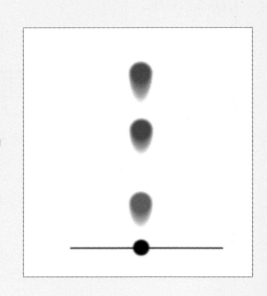

c Whose pen do you think was used to write the ransom note? Explain your answer.

d Give three reasons why this does not definitely prove who the kidnapper is.

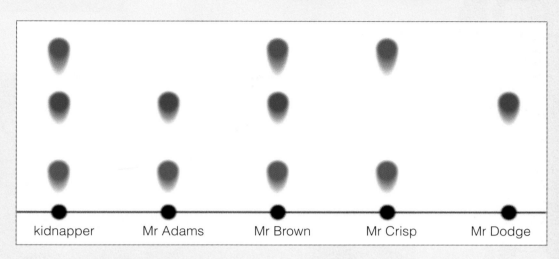

kidnapper Mr Adams Mr Brown Mr Crisp Mr Dodge

Analysing foods

Chromatography can also be used to look at the colourings in foods.

The Pluto Sweetie firm brought out a new range of sweets called Brighties. Tony was worried that the sweets might contain a colouring called sunburst yellow. Tony is allergic to sunburst yellow – it brings him out in big red spots. He can eat other yellow colours.

Tony used chromatography to separate out the colours in the orange and yellow sweets. He compared these with four different yellow food colours. His results are shown below.

Questions

Look at Tony's results and discuss the questions with your partner.

1. How many colours are in an orange Brightie?

2. What colours are they?

3. How many colours are in a yellow Brightie?

4. What colours are they?

5. What colour was not found in either of the sweets?

6. Will orange Brighties make Tony ill? Explain your answer.

7. Will yellow Brighties make Tony ill? Explain your answer.

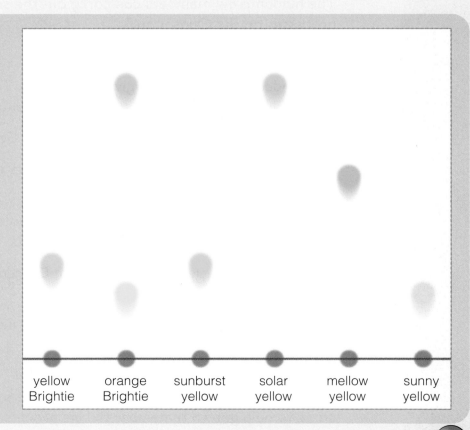

yellow Brightie | orange Brightie | sunburst yellow | solar yellow | mellow yellow | sunny yellow

Lookalikes

Human robots?

A new television programme called Quasar Quest 5 has robots that look exactly like humans. They walk and even talk like humans.

Zac235 is a robot and he assists Mr Zachariah. They look identical.

Looking after the crew

The human crew members can carry out the seven life processes on the Quasar ship.

- There is enough space for **M**ovement.

- Cylinders under the deck give out oxygen. The crew use this for **R**espiration, getting energy from food.

- Regular hearing and sight tests check out **S**ensitivity.

- Clothing is made from super stretch fabrics that stretch with **G**rowth.

- **R**eproduction will happen, babies will be born, so the nursery is specially equipped for the infants.

- The toilets recycle waste water from **E**xcretion for drinking and washing.

- **N**utrition is important, but all food has to be powdered to save space.

Mrs Gren is the flight attendant in charge of remembering all of this. You can use the letters in her name to help you to remember the life processes.

Did you know?

- On 17 December 1994, Pipin Ferreras dived underwater to a depth of 127 m with a single breath of air. He was under the water for 2 minutes 28 seconds!

- Human urine is 95% water.

- A dormouse goes to sleep in the autumn and wakes up in the spring with an enormous appetite!

Fact files

Read the fact files about Mr Zachariah and Zac235. The files give information about the things they can do.

(a) Make a list of Mr Zachariah's life processes.

FACT FILE: MR ZACHARIAH

MOVEMENT: CAN WALK AT A SPEED OF 3 KM/HOUR

BREATHING: BREATHES AIR

SENSORS: RESPONDS TO SOUND, LIGHT, TEMPERATURE CHANGES, CHEMICALS AND TOUCH

GROWTH: STOPPED AT A FINAL HEIGHT OF 2 METRES

FAMILY: IS THE FATHER OF TWO CHILDREN

DIET: INCLUDES CHICKEN, FISH, VEGETABLES AND FRUIT

SPECIAL REQUESTS: NEEDS TO HAVE A TOILET ON BOARD

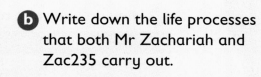

FACT FILE: ZAC235

MOVEMENT: CAN WALK AT A SPEED OF 3 KM/HOUR

BREATHING: NOT NECESSARY

SENSORS: RESPONDS TO SOUND, LIGHT, TEMPERATURE CHANGES, CHEMICALS AND TOUCH

GROWTH: FIXED SIZE

FAMILY: IS NOT POSSIBLE

DIET: NUCLEAR FUEL CELLS

SPECIAL REQUESTS: OIL CHANGE

(b) Write down the life processes that both Mr Zachariah and Zac235 carry out.

Questions

1. Some non-living things carry out some (but not all) of the life processes. Copy and complete these sentences using the words below.

> **breathe   feed   grow   move**

   a A robot and a human can both ...

   b A motorcycle and a mouse can both ...

   c A beech tree and a bank account can both ...

2. The crew of Quasar Quest 5 have found some green slime on one of Jupiter's moons. How can they test it to find out whether it is living or non-living?

Sorting out living things

Living things

Everything on Earth is either living or non-living.
We call living things **organisms**. The smallest living things are
called **microorganisms** and you need a microscope to see them.
Bacteria and **viruses** are microorganisms.

a How do we decide whether something is living or non-living?

Classifying organisms

We look at organisms and see what special parts they have or
what things they do. These are called their **features**. We put
organisms that have similar features into the same group. This
grouping is called **classification**.

The table shows how we start to classify living things.

b How do you start to classify living things?

Animals	Plants	Microorganisms	Fungi
Human	Lime tree	**Virus**	Toadstool
Horse			
	Primrose	**Bacterium**	Mould
Spider			
Feed on other animals or plants	Make their own food	**Can only be seen with a microscope**	Feed on rotting material
Most move around	Green		

Wherever you look, you will find examples of all these groups. You will
find animals, plants, microorganisms and fungi in soil or in a pond. There
are many different living things even in very cold places like the Arctic.

Animal X-rays

seal

All the animals are put into two groups, those with a backbone and those without a backbone.

Here are some X-rays of animals from the Arctic.

c Look at the X-rays. Which of these animals have a backbone?

cod

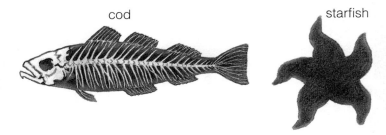

starfish

We call animals with backbones **vertebrates**. We call animals without backbones **invertebrates**.

octopus

crab

arctic tern

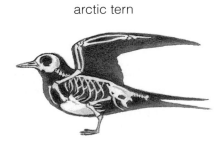

Questions

1. Copy and complete these sentences by choosing from the words below.

> **big   bigger   different   groups**
> **organisms   similar   small   smaller**

We can sort living things into _____. All of the _____ in a group have _____ features. Each _____ group can be sorted into _____ groups.

2. Copy the table below. Write the following animals in the correct column. You are classifying them.

> **human   horse   polar bear**
> **octopus   spider   starfish   cod**

Vertebrates	Invertebrates

For your notes

We can sort living things into groups with similar **features**. This is called **classification**.

Vertebrates are animals with a backbone.

Invertebrates are animals without a backbone.

More animal groups

Five groups of vertebrates

The vertebrates are divided into five smaller groups.

Mammals	Birds	Reptiles	Amphibians	Fish
Lion	Eagle	Crocodile	Frog	Shark

a Where do you think humans fit in?

Sort yourself out

Humans have a backbone, so we are **vertebrates**. We are classified as **mammals**. Lions, apes, dogs, cats and many other furry animals are also mammals.

Mammals

These are the features of mammals:

- Their babies develop inside the mother's body.
- The mother feeds the young on her milk, which she makes in her **mammary glands**.
- They have hairy skin.

The rest of the vertebrates apart from mammals are classified as:

- birds
- reptiles
- amphibians
- fish.

> **Did you know?**
> Mammals, birds, reptiles and amphibians breathe air using lungs.

> **Did you know?**
> Mammals and birds are the only groups of vertebrates that look after their young. Reptiles, amphibians and fish usually leave their young to fend for themselves.

Birds

b Which features of birds are used for movement?

- **Birds** lay eggs with a hard shell.
- They look after their young after they have hatched.
- Birds have feathers and wings.
- Most birds can fly.

Reptiles

c Look at the photo. Describe a crocodile's skin.

- **Reptiles** lay eggs on land. Their eggs have a leathery shell.
- They breathe air and live mainly on land.
- They have a scaly, dry skin.

Amphibians

- **Amphibians** lay eggs in water. The eggs are like jelly.
- They breathe air and live partly on land, but have to lay their eggs in water.
- They have a smooth, moist skin.

d Why do you think salamanders go back to water in the spring?

Fish

e How do you think a salmon breathes?

- **Fish** can only live in water. They lay eggs in water.
- They breathe through gills.
- They have scales and fins.

Questions

1. Copy and complete the table.

Vertebrate group	Features
Mammals	Have mammary glands, babies develop inside mother's body, have hairy skin
	Lay eggs with a hard shell, have feathers and wings
Reptiles	
Amphibians	
	Lay eggs, live in water, breathe through gills, have scales and fins

2. Where do reptiles live and reproduce, on land or in water?

3. Which group of vertebrates feeds its young on milk?

For your notes

Vertebrates are classified into five groups.

The groups are **mammals**, **birds**, **reptiles**, **amphibians** and **fish**.

Each group has different features.

Make no bones about it

Invertebrates

The invertebrate animals have no backbones. We start to classify them by their legs. They have no legs or lots of legs.

No legs

We can start to sort the invertebrates with no legs into groups by the kind of body they have – hard or soft. There are six groups.

Invertebrate group		Body
Jellyfish		Soft jelly-like body
Starfish		Hard star-shaped body
Flatworms		Soft flat leaf-shaped body
Roundworms		Soft thin round body
Segmented worms		Soft ringed body
Molluscs		Soft muscular body with one foot. Most have a hard shell.

a What feature do we use to classify invertebrates with no legs?

b In which group is an earthworm? It has no legs and a soft body with rings.

Jointed legs

We call the invertebrates with lots of jointed legs **arthropods**. The Latin word for foot is *pod*. Arthropods have bodies made of sections called **segments**.

We divide the arthropods into four smaller groups:

Arthropod group		Number of legs	Body
Crustaceans	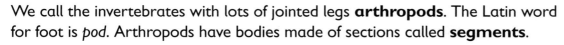	Lots of legs	Soft body, usually with a hard shell
Centipedes and millipedes		Lots of legs	Segmented body
Spiders		8 legs	2-part segmented body
Insects		6 legs	3-part segmented body

c What is an arthropod?

d What is the difference between a centipede and a roundworm?

Did you know?
There are three times as many kinds of insect on the Earth as all the other animals put together.

Questions

1. Copy and complete these sentences by choosing from the words below.

> jellyfish starfish flatworm roundworm
> segmented worm mollusc arthropod
> crustacean spider insect millipede centipede

I have a flat leaf-shaped body and no legs. I am a ...

I have a star-shaped body. I am a ...

I have lots of legs and a shell. I am a ...

2. How can you tell the difference between an insect and a spider?

For your notes

Invertebrates are classified into seven groups.

The groups are **jellyfish, starfish, flatworms, roundworms, segmented worms, molluscs** and **arthropods**.

The arthropod group is divided into **crustaceans, centipedes and millipedes, spiders** and **insects**.

Differences count

Species

We group living things together by the similar features they have. However, there are also differences within groups of living things.

If there are enough differences, we call them different **species**. Wolves and reindeer are both mammals, but different species. They cannot mate to produce a baby 'wolfdeer' or 'reinolf'!

Wolf   *Reindeer*

The same but different

The humans in this crowd all belong to the same species because they have many similarities.

a In what ways are the people in this crowd the same?

No two people are exactly alike – not even identical twins!

b In what ways are the people in this crowd different?

We are all different

We all belong to the species called humans. We have different coloured eyes and hair. We have different weights and heights. Some of us are cleverer than others. Some of us are better at sport. Differences like these are called **variation**.

We are all different because different features are passed on to us from our parents. These are **inherited features**. We are also different because we have grown up in different **surroundings**. For example, eating the wrong sort of food can make people fatter.

c Give another way in which our surroundings or how we are brought up can affect the way we look.

Questions

1. Copy and complete these sentences by choosing from the words below.

> **inherited   parents   surroundings**
> **differences   species   variations**

There are _____ between members of the same _____. These differences are called _____. Some of these differences are inherited from the _____. Differences in the _____ or upbringing also cause variation.

2. Why do you think that you cannot mate a polar bear with a seal, but you can mate a polar bear with a brown bear?

For your notes

We call the differences between living things **variation**.

If there are enough differences between organisms, they are different **species**.

Some variations between the members of a species are **inherited** from their parents, and some are caused by their **surroundings**.

43

Born to survive

Paws for thought

A polar bear goes out without a care
of what clothes he should wear.
With only his thick white coat
– not even a scarf around his throat!
His colour is white to hide in the snow
from hunters he does not know.
Sitting on the edge of the ice,
a sight of dinner would be nice.
If a seal appears, he is ready to stalk –
no time to bother with a knife and fork!

a Make a list of the features of a polar
bear that help it to survive in the Arctic.

Learn about

► Adaptation

Adaptation

The place where an animal lives is called its **habitat**. The polar
bear's habitat is the Arctic. The polar bear has a thick coat made of
hollow hair. This helps it survive in the cold North Pole snow and in
the freezing Arctic sea with its packed ice. Having features that are
suited to a habitat is called **adaptation**.

Camouflage

The polar bear's coat is white, so it
does not show up against the snow.
Other animals, including humans,
cannot see the polar bear very
easily. We call this **camouflage**.
This is another adaptation. A baby
seal also has a white coat, so it
cannot be seen in the snow. The
adult seal grows a short, sleek, black
coat that gives better camouflage
against the dark sea.

b What does camouflage mean?

Other adaptations

Many animals can **adapt** (change) to cope with different seasons and weather.

In the Arctic there are foxes, hares, caribou (reindeer) and long-haired cattle called musk. They all have long hair or thick fur to keep them warm. The arctic fox and the arctic hare grow longer white fur for the winter. This hair falls out in the summer. This is called **moulting**.

In the Arctic sea there are seals and whales. They have a thick layer of fat called **blubber** to keep them warm.

The other extreme

Unlike the Arctic, the Sahara desert is very hot during the day. At night it is very cold. Animals that live in the desert must be adapted to changes in temperature and very dry conditions.

In the desert, some animals change their behaviour with the temperature.

Gerbils burrow into the desert sand to avoid the midday heat.

c Why do gerbils burrow in the sand?

d Look at the photo on the left. Why is the lizard sheltering under the rock?

Questions

1. Copy and complete these sentences by choosing from the words below.

> **adapted   cold   fat   fur   sun   thick   warm   white**

Polar bears and seals are _____ to survive in the cold.

Polar bears have a _____ coat. Seals have _____ called blubber. Both of these help to keep them _____ in winter.

In the desert, gerbils burrow into the sand to shelter from the midday _____.

For your notes

Many animals are **adapted** to survive in their **habitat**.

Some animals are adapted to survive in the cold. They have fur or fat to keep them warm.

Some animals are **camouflaged** to hide from other animals.

Some animals change their behaviour to help them cope with changes in temperature.

45

Eskimo pen pal

Biork lives in Alaska, close to the Arctic Circle.
Biork's ancestors are called Eskimos or Inuit people.
Biork's people have survived the cold Arctic conditions for
thousands of years. Biork's grandfather used to go out
hunting for seals. He wore clothes made out of animal
skins and built overnight shelters out of ice to keep warm.

*Inuit people
are born with short
compact bodies. It's a feature
that has been passed on
through our families.*

Why are Inuit people small?

The Inuit people have short, heavy, compact
bodies. Biork has often wondered why she
is small. She would like to be tall and thin
like her pen friend in Florida. Biork's
grandfather says it's a feature that helps
them keep warm.

a What do you think makes the Inuits
have short, heavy, compact bodies?

Biork's body shape is inherited from her
parents, but it also depends on her
surroundings, lifestyle and upbringing.
Lots of variables can affect our height
and weight. Some of these are:

● food

● exercise

● seasons

● illness

● stress.

Research

A group of Canadian scientists studied the heights of more than 150 Inuit children. They compared them with a sample of 150 children in the USA. The diagram shows what might happen if the sample size is too small.

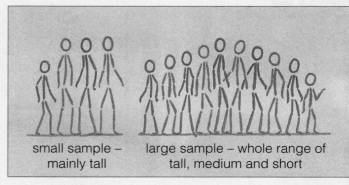

small sample – mainly tall   large sample – whole range of tall, medium and short

b Why do you think it is better to study a sample of 150 children from each place rather than only 10?

c How would you choose the children that you were going to study?

Making comparisons

When they had collected their figures, the scientists compared the tallest in each sample and the smallest in each sample. They did this to see the differences.

Analysing the results

The graph shows the data for the Inuit girls compared with girls in the USA.

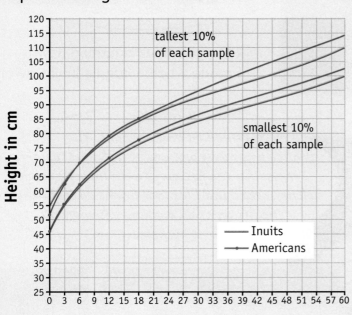

Age in months

When both groups of children are 12 months old, the lines on the graph for the Inuit children and the American children are close together. This means that their heights are similar. After this, the lines are further apart, showing that the American children are taller.

Questions

1. Discuss the graph with your partner. Copy and complete these sentences together by choosing from the words below.

faster   large   slower   small

There is a _____ difference in the heights of the Inuits and American girls when they are 12 months old.

As they get older, the gap widens. The Inuit girls grew _____ than the girls in the USA.

2. What other data should the scientists collect and analyse to check whether the Inuits' small size is inherited? Explain why you made your suggestions.

The burning question

Bonfire night

> I'm looking forward to the bonfire at the community centre. People have been piling up the branches and twigs for days. All of my family are going and so is my friend Deepak and his family.

> My family will be celebrating Divali, the festival of light. During the festival of light, my mum lights a candle on the window sill.

a Do you think anything new is made when a candle burns away?

> Last year it rained on bonfire night. The bonfire was really wet and it took ages to light. I remember the fireworks with their dancing colours, green and lilac and bright white flashes. The fire was still burning when we all went home.

This bonfire is brilliant, better than last year. Even back behind the rope I can feel the heat of the flames on my cold face.

I wish we could go closer.

Most of the wood has burned away since last night. It's a pity you can't get it all back for next year.

b What do you think was left?

Questions

1. Look at the word wall very carefully.

heat	ash	reversible	material
change	flame	new	burning	air

Try using the words to finish these sentences:

a When a **material** burns, we see a …

b **Burning** is a **change** that is not …

c For a **material** to burn, you need to give it …

Choose two or three words and arrange them together with linking words to make a new sentence. Here is an example to help you:

● When a **material** burns it leaves **ash**.

Try again to see how many sentences you can make. You will be surprised how much you already know about burning!

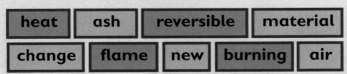

49

How does it happen?

Oxygen

Is air needed for burning? Look at the picture. Three jars of different sizes are placed over a burning candle.

candle went out after 10 seconds

candle went out after 8 seconds

candle went out after 4 seconds

Ⓐ Which candle burned for the longest time?

The candle under the biggest jar burned for the longest time. This jar had the most air inside it. A candle needs air to burn.

Burning uses up part of the air. There is a mixture of gases that you cannot see in the air. One of these gases is used up by burning materials. It is the same gas that we need to stay alive.

Ⓑ What is the gas in the air that we need to stay alive?

The gas in the air that is used up when materials burn is **oxygen**.

Firefighting

Firefighters sometimes have a cylinder of oxygen on their backs, so that they can breathe in a burning building. The fire in the building uses up the oxygen.

Flammable materials

Some materials burn more easily than others. These are called **flammable materials**.

c Try and think of any materials you have seen or used in the laboratory that are flammable.

Substances that are flammable have a hazard warning label on the container to warn people of the danger.

The fire triangle

In a fire, the burning material is acting as a **fuel**. A fuel gives out lots of energy as heat and light when it burns.

d How do you think dangerous fires start?

You need three things to make a fire burn:

- fuel
- oxygen
- heat.

These are shown in the fire triangle. To put a fire out, you have to break the triangle by taking away the fuel, the oxygen or the heat.

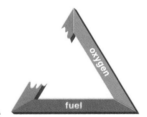

Questions

1. Copy and complete these sentences using the words below.

> **flammable   gas   heat   oxygen**

Materials that burn easily are called _____.
The _____ in the air used in burning is called
_____. To put a fire out, you must take away
the fuel, the _____ or the _____.

2. Draw the flammable hazard warning symbol.

3. Draw the fire triangle.

4. Firefighters often put fires out with water. Which part of the fire triangle are they taking away?

For your notes

The part of the air needed for burning is called **oxygen**. Oxygen is also needed for life.

Flammable materials burn more easily than others.

Fires need fuel, oxygen and heat to burn.

Burning changes

Chemical change

Have you ever looked at what is left from a bonfire next day?

a Look at the photo opposite. What does it look like?

After a bonfire, all that remains is ash and soot. You cannot get the wood back from the ash – burning is an irreversible change. Burning is a **chemical change**. When a chemical change happens, you cannot get back the substance you started with.

Oxides

The substances left behind in the ash are called **oxides**. When a substance burns, it joins with oxygen in the air to make an oxide. The name 'oxide' comes from the word 'oxygen'. We take the first two letters of oxygen and add 'ide'.

Fireworks

Metals burn to make oxides. We use metals in fireworks because they give out flashes, sparks and colours.

Magnesium

Magnesium is a silvery coloured metal. It burns to give a white flash which is very bright. You have to look at it through blue glass or it will damage your eyes.

Flash bulbs for cameras have magnesium inside them. When magnesium burns it leaves a white powder called **magnesium oxide**.

Iron

When iron burns, it gives out sparks. Fireworks like the sparkler opposite have iron powder in them. The name of the new substance is **iron oxide**.

Copper

Look at the photo opposite. Copper becomes coated with a black substance when you hold it in a flame. When you burn substances that have copper in them, the flame looks greenish.

b What do you think the black substance is?

The copper joins with the oxygen in the air to make **copper oxide**.

Questions

1. Why are metals used in fireworks?

2. Write down what happens when you burn:

   a magnesium

   b iron

   c copper.

For your notes

Substances join with oxygen to make **oxides**. This is a **chemical change**.

Some metals burn in air to make oxides.

Useful burning

Fuels store energy

A **fuel** is a substance that stores a lot of chemical energy. When the fuel burns, it releases **heat energy** or **light energy** which we can use. The human body uses food as a fuel.

Jenny's holiday diary

Friday
Dad spent all day packing the car before we set off. Mum made him go to the garage and fill up with petrol because she didn't want to run out before we got to the ferry port.

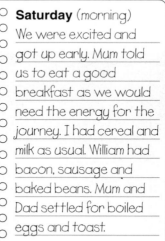

Saturday (morning)
We were excited and got up early. Mum told us to eat a good breakfast as we would need the energy for the journey. I had cereal and milk as usual. William had bacon, sausage and baked beans. Mum and Dad settled for boiled eggs and toast.

Saturday (lunchtime)
There was an enormous queue on the ferry boat for cooked lunch, so we only had a sandwich from the snack bar.

Saturday (evening)
It was 9 o'clock in the evening when we finally reached the camp site because we got lost and couldn't get any gas for the camping stove. William was so hungry that he ate his last bar of chocolate. I just fell asleep ...

(a) Make a list of all the fuels Jenny mentioned. (Hint: include foods.)

(b) Which fuel shown is used to give out: **i** movement energy? **ii** light energy?

How much energy is in food?

When we eat food, the body uses it as fuel. Food gives us energy to keep warm and move around.

We measure energy in **joules**, **J**. There are 1000 J in 1 **kilojoule**, **kJ**. Different foods contain different amounts of energy. Sausages contain much more energy than breakfast cereal.

How much energy is in fuels?

We burn different fuels to keep warm, light our houses and roads or make things move. Different fuels give out different amounts of energy. A small piece of coal gives out more energy than a small piece of wood. The pictures show some different fuels being used.

c Make a list of the different fuels shown in the pictures. Can you think of any others to add?

candle

barbecue

camping gas

petrol

Barbecue time

The fuel for a barbecue is charcoal. Charcoal is a fuel because it has a store of energy. This **chemical energy** stays in the charcoal until you light it. When the charcoal burns, the energy comes out as heat energy and light energy.

d What is happening to the energy from the burning charcoal?

The heat energy is transferred from the charcoal to the food, making it hot.

Questions

1. Copy and complete these sentences using the words below.

   | burns   chemical   heat   light   stores |

   A fuel _____ energy. We call this
   _____ energy. When a fuel _____,
   the stored energy is released as _____
   energy and _____ energy.

2. Read Jenny's diary.

   a Who ate the most food for breakfast?

   b Who ate the least food for breakfast?

   c Who gained the most energy from their breakfast?

For your notes

Fuels store energy. Energy is released when fuels burn. There are many different fuels.

The body uses food as fuel.

We measure energy in **joules, J**.

55

What's special about fuels?

Before and after

In the days before central heating, most people lit a fire every morning. First they screwed up some paper, and then placed wooden sticks on top. Finally they put on a few lumps of coal and lit the paper with a match.

The paper started the wood burning, and then the coal started to burn. The coal burned steadily, giving out the most heat energy.

a What do you think was left next morning?

No one liked clearing up next day. Cleaning out the grey ash was a messy job.

Coal

Some people still have coal fires in their homes. Coal is a black, shiny, rocky substance.

b Where does coal come from?

Coal comes from dead trees. The trees were squashed under the ground and gradually changed to coal. This took millions of years. Coal has to be dug out of the ground by coal miners.

Carbon

Coal is mainly **carbon**. When carbon burns, it joins with oxygen in the air to make an oxide of carbon called **carbon dioxide**. Other fuels contain carbon. Wood, gas, charcoal and petrol all produce carbon dioxide when they burn. Food also has carbon in it. When your body uses food as fuel, it gives you energy and carbon dioxide is made.

> ### Did you know?
>
> We mine 3000 million tonnes of coal each year. At this rate coal will last for about 300 years before it is all used up.

Carbon dioxide

Carbon dioxide is an invisible gas. Unlike oxygen, carbon dioxide is not needed for burning. It puts fires out!

You can test for carbon dioxide with a solution called **limewater**. First you have to collect the gas. You collect it in a funnel and pass it along a tube into the limewater. As the carbon dioxide gas bubbles through the limewater, it turns milky white.

Questions

1. Copy and complete these sentences using the words below.

> burns   carbon   gas   joins   oxide
> carbon dioxide

Most fuels contain _____. When carbon _____, it _____ with oxygen to make an _____ of carbon. This is a _____ called _____.

2. How can we show that carbon dioxide is made when a lump of coal burns?

For your notes

The fuels we burn contain **carbon**, and so does food.

When carbon burns, it joins with oxygen in the air to make **carbon dioxide**.

Carbon dioxide is a gas which turns **limewater** milky.

It's all about reactions

Particles

Coal is mainly carbon. Carbon is made of carbon particles. Oxygen is made of oxygen particles. Coal burns when you light it. Each carbon particle joins with two oxygen particles to make carbon dioxide. Carbon dioxide is a new substance.

oxygen particle   carbon particle

carbon dioxide

Chemical reactions

When different particles join together to make new substances, we call it a **chemical reaction**. Burning is a chemical reaction. The chemical name for burning is **combustion**.

On the left are one carbon particle and two oxygen particles.   They react and join together.   On the right is carbon dioxide made from one carbon particle and two oxygen particles joined together.

a What chemical reaction is taking place in a coal fire?

b Which new substance is made when carbon burns?

In science, we write a **word equation** to show what happens in a reaction.

> carbon + oxygen → carbon dioxide

In maths, we write equations to show what happens when you add numbers together. There are the same number of balls on both sides of the equation.

In a chemical reaction, there are the same number of particles on both sides of the equation. The mass is the same on both sides.

Burning other fuels

We have already seen that some fuels, such as coal, are mostly carbon. When they burn they produce carbon dioxide.

Fuels such as wax, petrol and oil are called **hydrocarbons**. The 'hydro' part means they contain hydrogen as well as carbon. Food also contains hydrogen. When hydrocarbons burn, the carbon joins with oxygen to produce carbon dioxide. The hydrogen also joins with oxygen to produce 'hydrogen oxide', which we know as water.

We can write a word equation for this part of the reaction:

> hydrogen + oxygen → water

Petrol and oil are both hydrocarbons.

Questions

1. Copy and complete these sentences by choosing from the words below.

> **bigger   carbon   join   particles   smaller**

When coal burns, oxygen _____ in the air _____ with particles of carbon in the coal. They make _____ particles of a new substance called _____ dioxide.

2. Copy and complete the word equation.

carbon + oxygen →

For your notes

When a fuel burns, a **chemical reaction** called **combustion** takes place.

A **word equation** shows what happens in a chemical reaction.

Hydrocarbons are fuels that contain carbon and hydrogen.

Getting hotter

Fuels in industry

We burn large amounts of fuels such as coal, oil and gas. This gives light energy and heat energy, and energy to make things move. The more fuels we burn, the more carbon dioxide we release into the air.

The greenhouse effect

The carbon dioxide in the air has the same effect as the glass in a greenhouse. The glass stops some of the heat energy in the greenhouse escaping, and the plants stay warm. Carbon dioxide stops some of the heat energy from the Earth escaping, and the Earth stays warm. This is called the **greenhouse effect**.

Scientists think that the greenhouse effect may make the Earth too hot as we produce more and more carbon dioxide.

Think about

➤ Relationships between variables

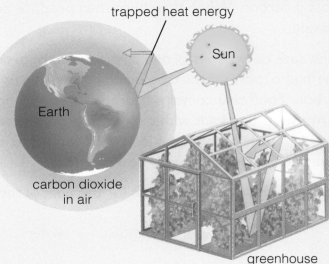

trapped heat energy

Sun

Earth

carbon dioxide in air

greenhouse

a What stops some of the heat energy escaping from the Earth?

b Why do we call this the greenhouse effect?

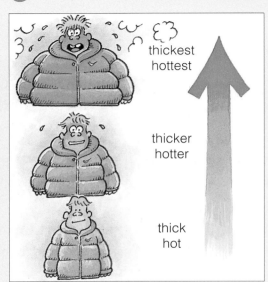

thickest hottest

thicker hotter

thick hot

The layer of carbon dioxide in the air acts like a quilted jacket. The thicker the quilt, the hotter you are!

c Copy and complete this sentence to show what we think the **relationship** is between the temperature of the Earth and the carbon dioxide in the air:
As the amount of carbon dioxide increases, the Earth gets …

d What do you think would happen if the amount of carbon dioxide in the air decreased?

The biodome experiment

A team of students decided to find out whether the temperature of the Earth rises when the level of carbon dioxide increases.

They set up a biodome. This is a **model** of the Earth. Carbon dioxide can be added through the tube at the side. The carbon dioxide level and the temperature inside the dome were recorded by a computer.

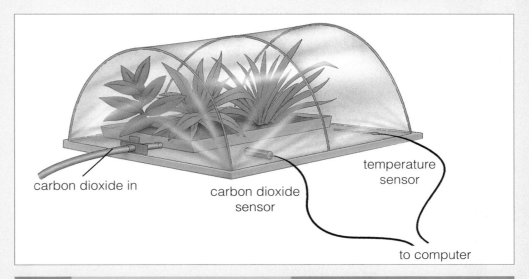

carbon dioxide in

carbon dioxide sensor

temperature sensor

to computer

Any relationship?

e What is the input variable in this experiment?

f What is the outcome variable?

We use the word **relationship** to describe how the outcome variable changes when we change the input variable.

The students increased the level of carbon dioxide each day for 5 days. They recorded the temperature inside the dome during that time to see if there was a relationship between carbon dioxide level and temperature. Their results are shown in the table.

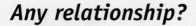

Day	Input variable Carbon dioxide level in %	Outcome variable Temperature in °C
1	0.1	20
2	0.2	21
3	0.3	22
4	0.4	23
5	0.5	24

Questions

1. Look at the table above. Copy and complete these sentences by choosing from the words in bold.

   a Both the carbon dioxide level and the temperature in the biodome have **increased/decreased** over the 5 days.

   b As the carbon dioxide level **increased/decreased**, the temperature became **high/higher**.

2. Find out how the greenhouse effect could change our weather.

At the touch of a switch

Life without light bulbs

Imagine life without electricity. There would be no television or computers. There would be no washing machines or microwaves.

a How many times did you use electricity this morning? Make a list.

Imagine life without electric light.

b Describe what it would be like doing your homework by candlelight.

The filament lamp

The electric light bulb is a **filament lamp**. There is a piece of wire called a filament inside the glass bulb. The electricity heats the wire, and the wire glows and gives out light.

c What heats the filament?

d What happens when the filament heats up?

Using different filaments

Humphry Davy made light using electricity in 1801. He put strips of platinum in a circuit. Unfortunately, the metal burned, so the light went out.

e What went wrong with Humphry Davy's lamp?

Humphry Davy.

Joseph Swan.

In 1850 Joseph Swan tried filaments of paper covered with carbon, but the filament burned away in the air. The lamp would only work if the filament was kept away from air.

Joseph Swan made a successful light bulb in 1878, followed closely by Thomas Edison in 1879. The trick was to take the air out of the bulb so the filament did not burn. These first light bulbs had carbon filaments.

In 1911 the carbon filament was changed to a tungsten filament. The tungsten filament lasted longer. In 1913 the filaments were changed to coiled filaments. This meant there was more wire to glow.

f Why was the tungsten filament better than the carbon filament?

g Why was the coiled filament better than a straight filament?

Questions

1. How is an electric filament lamp better than a candle?

2. Electric filament bulbs:
   - give out bright light
   - give out a lot of heat energy
   - are cheap
   - break when dropped
   - 'blow' after they have been used for a long time.

   a What are the good points of an electric filament bulb?

   b How could the electric filament bulb be improved?

3. Streetlights used to be gas lamps. A person called a lamplighter used to light the lamps each evening and turn them out each morning. Imagine you are a lamplighter. All the streetlights are being changed to electricity. You will lose your job. Write a letter to a friend about how you feel.

Circuit training

Learn about

➤ Circuits

Energy from electricity

Electricity carries energy to make things work.

In the picture, the battery is making the lamp light.

Electricity carries energy to make things work.

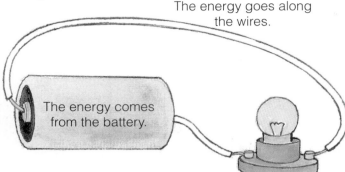

The energy goes along the wires.

The energy comes from the battery.

The lamp transfers light energy and heat energy.

a Look at the diagram below. It shows an energy transfer. Copy and complete the diagram using the words below.

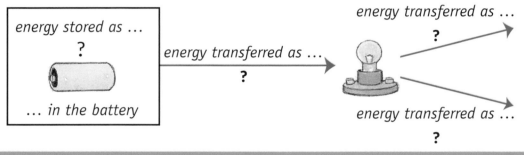

energy stored as ...

?

... in the battery

energy transferred as ...

?

energy transferred as ...

?

energy transferred as ...

?

| electrical energy | heat energy | chemical energy | light energy |

Making connections

You can join batteries and a lamp in many different ways.

b Look at the drawings below. Which lamp will light up?

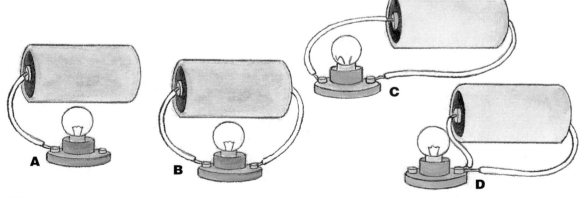

A

B

C

D

The battery, the wires and the lamp have to be connected to make a **complete circuit**. Lamp **A** is missing a wire to join the lamp back to the battery. Lamp **D** is not in the circuit. Lamp **C** has a broken filament, so the circuit is broken.

You need a complete circuit to make a lamp light.

Circuit symbols

We use simple symbols to show batteries, lamps and switches.

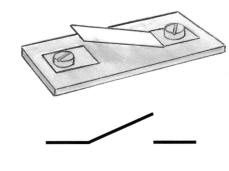

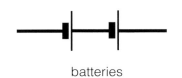

batteries

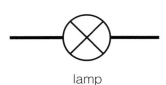

lamp

switch

Questions

1. Draw circuit **X** shown opposite using symbols.

circuit **X**

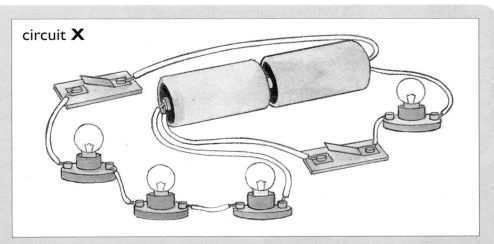

2. Look at circuit **Y**. All the switches are shown open.

circuit **Y**

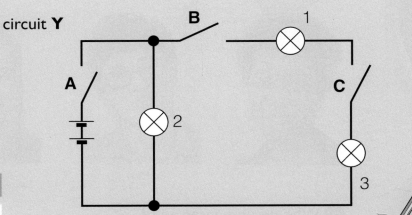

 a How many lamps are there in this circuit?

 b How many switches are there in this circuit?

 c Copy and complete this table.

Switches closed	Lamps lit
A, B, C	1, 2, 3
None	
A, C	
A, B	
A	

For your notes

We get energy from electricity to make things work.

You need a **complete circuit** for energy to be transferred.

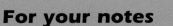

Current

Wires join the battery to the lamp. Electricity flows in the wires. We call this a **current** in the wires. We measure the current with an **ammeter**. The ammeter isput into the circuit.

An ammeter measures current in **amps**. The short way of writing amps is **A**. The circuit symbol for an ammeter is (**A**).

a Where do you put the ammeter to measure the current?

b What is current measured in?

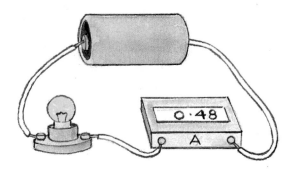

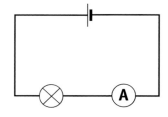

Moving the ammeter

You can move the ammeter to different parts of the circuit. The teacher asked Ben, Laura and Dan what would happen.

Is the current the same on both sides of the lamp?

It will be more on the right of the lamp.

It will be more on the left of the lamp.

It will be the same on both sides of the lamp.

Ben

Laura

Dan

c Who do you agree with?

They did the experiment to check their prediction. It is shown here.

d Who was right?

The current is the same on both sides of the lamp.

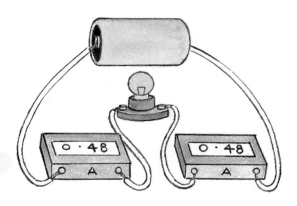

More complicated circuits

Ben and Lucy decided to investigate this question:

• If you have more batteries, does the current change?

I think the lamps will get brighter, but I think the current will stay the same.

I think the lamps will get brighter and the current will increase.

Look at the circuits they used below, and their results.

e Who was correct, Ben or Lucy?

f Describe the relationship between the number of batteries and the current.

Ben   Lucy

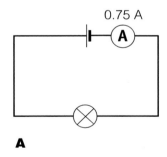

0.75 A

A

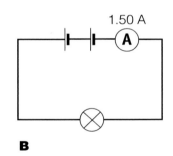

1.50 A

B

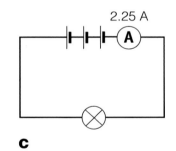

2.25 A

C

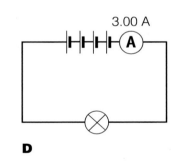

3.00 A

D

Questions

1. Copy and complete these sentences.

There is a current in the _____. We measure current using an _____. Current is measured in _____. The current is the _____ before and after a lamp.

2. Look at the results from Ben and Lucy's experiment.

  a Which lamp will be brightest?

  b Why will this lamp be brightest?

  c Ben and Lucy did not use five or six batteries. Suggest why they stopped at four.

For your notes

Current is measured in **amps, A,** using an **ammeter**.

The current is the same on both sides of a lamp.

Increasing the number of batteries makes the lamps brighter and increases the current.

Voltage

We have learned about current. Current is measured *in* the circuit using an ammeter. The ammeter is put *in* the circuit.

We can also measure **voltage**.

Voltage tells us the change in the energy in the circuit. Voltage is not measured *in* the circuit. It is measured *across* parts of the circuit. Voltage is measured with a **voltmeter**. The voltmeter is put *across* parts of the circuit.

Voltage is measured in **volts**. The short way of writing volts is **V**. The circuit symbol for a voltmeter is (V).

Energy in and out

Ben and Lucy measured the voltage across four parts of a circuit. The circuit is shown using black wires. The wires going to the voltmeters are in pink. The circuit diagram shows the same circuit.

a Do they get a voltage across:
   i the lamp?
   ii the battery?
   iii the wires?

There is a voltage across the lamp. Energy leaves the circuit at the lamp. It leaves as light energy and heat energy.

There is a voltage across the battery. Energy goes into the circuit at the battery. Batteries put electrical energy into the circuit.

There is no voltage across the wires. No energy goes in or out of the circuit at the wires.

b Where does energy go into the circuit?

c Where does energy leave the circuit?

d Why is there no voltage across the wires?

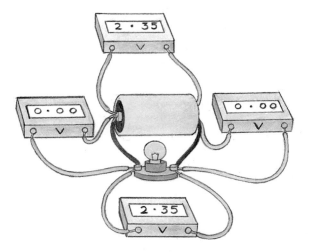

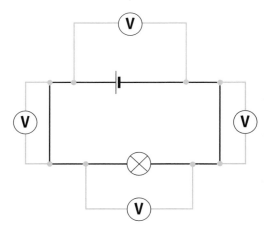

There is a voltage across any part of a circuit where energy goes into the circuit or where energy leaves the circuit.

Batteries and voltage

Batteries put energy into circuits. If you connect a voltmeter across a battery, it will show a voltage.

Ellen and Jermaine investigated how increasing the number of batteries changed the voltage. They made three circuits, **A**, **B** and **C**. The batteries were all the same. The lamps were all the same.

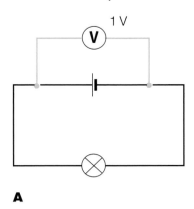
A

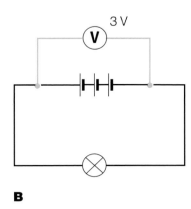
B

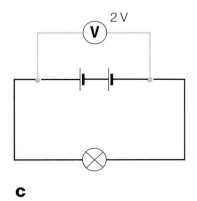
C

e Which voltmeter shows the biggest reading? Why?

f Which circuit has the most energy going in?

g Which lamp would be brightest?

h Ellen made another circuit with four batteries. Predict the reading on the voltmeter.

Questions

1. Draw a circuit diagram with a battery, a lamp, an ammeter and a voltmeter across the lamp.

2. There were three lamps in a circuit. The lamps were not the same. Seth measured the voltage across each lamp.

Lamp	Voltage in V
A	1.0
B	3.0
C	2.0

Which lamp gives out the most energy?

For your notes

Voltage is measured across parts of a circuit.

Voltage is measured in **volts**, **V**, using a **voltmeter**.

There is a voltage across any part of the circuit where energy is entering or exiting.

Models of electricity

Using models

Scientists use **models** to help them think.
Each part of a model stands for something in real life.

A good model fits with the facts. So far, you know these facts about electricity.

> Electricity carries energy to make things work.

> You need a complete circuit to make a lamp light.

> The current is the same on both sides of the lamp.

> There is a voltage across any part of a circuit where energy goes into the circuit or where energy leaves the circuit.

The coal truck model

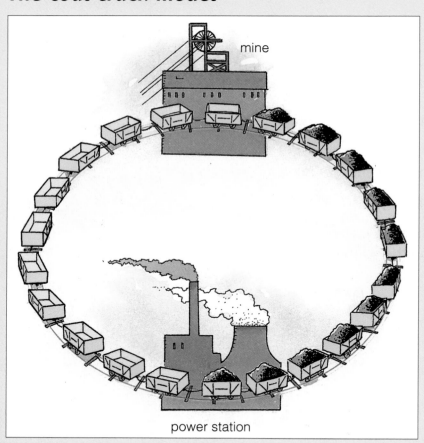

mine

power station

This model shows a mine and a power station. There is a single-track railway between the mine and the power station. Coal trucks run along the railway. The coal trucks can move quickly or slowly along the track.

At the mine, the coal trucks are filled with coal. The coal trucks run along the tracks and deliver the coal to the power station. The empty coal trucks then return to the mine.

Read the description carefully again and study the diagram.
Then answer the questions.

a In the coal truck model, what stands for:

  i the circuit? **ii** the battery? **iii** the lamp? **iv** the energy?

b The moving trucks represent the current. The trucks speed up.
Has the current increased or decreased?

c Do you think there is anything in the model about voltage?

The class and matches model

Mrs Fuller is using another model to explain electricity to her class.

Mrs Fuller gives each pupil a match as they pass her.

The pupils continue and collect another match.

The pupils carry their matches round the white circle.

Mrs Huxley strikes each match as the pupil passes it to her.

d Think about this model. What stands for:

   i the energy?

   ii the circuit?

   iii the current?

   iv the voltage?

e Draw a diagram of this model. Use the same colours as in the coal truck model:

- energy is green
- the circuit is pink
- the current is yellow
- the voltage (where energy enters and exits) is blue.

Questions

1. Jackie and Lester drew diagrams to show the class and matches model of electricity.

   a Does Jackie's diagram show what happens in a circuit? Explain your answer.

   b Does Lester's diagram show what happens in a circuit? Explain your answer.

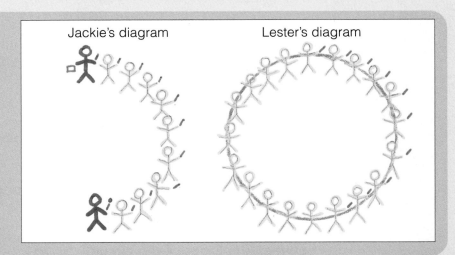

Jackie's diagram   Lester's diagram

More circuits

Series and parallel circuits

There are two ways of connecting two lamps and a battery.

You can put the lamps side by side, as shown here.

This is called a **series** circuit.

You can put the lamps in different loops, as here.

This is called a **parallel** circuit.

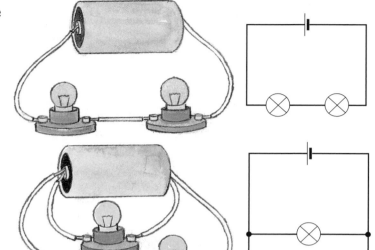

Suzy and John compared series and parallel circuits. They used identical batteries and identical lamps. The lamps were brighter in the parallel circuit.

a Which circuit has the lamps side by side?

b Which circuit has the lamps in different loops?

c Which lamps are brighter?

Current in series and parallel circuits

series circuit

parallel circuit

Kimberly and Jason built these circuits. They measured the current at different points in each circuit.

In the series circuit, the current was the same at all points in the circuit. In the parallel circuit, the current was shared between the loops of the circuit.

d Look at the series circuit. What would the current be at **X** and at **Y**?

e Look at the parallel circuit. What would the current be at **P**, at **Q** and at **R**?

Voltage in series and parallel circuits

Moomith and Alan built these circuits. They measured the voltage across the battery and across each lamp.

In the series circuit, they found that the voltage across the battery is shared between the lamps. In the parallel circuit, they found that the voltage was the same across the battery and each lamp.

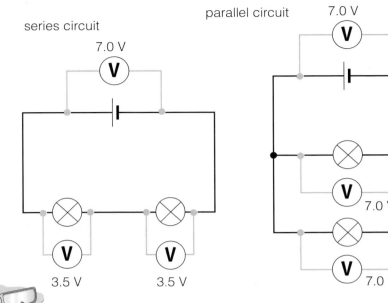

series circuit

7.0 V

3.5 V   3.5 V

parallel circuit   7.0 V

7.0 V

7.0 V

f In which circuit is the voltage across the battery shared between the lamps?

g In which circuit are the voltmeter readings all the same?

Questions

1. Read these statements.

- The lamps are brighter.
- The lamps are dimmer.
- The voltage is the same across the battery and each lamp.
- The voltage across the battery is shared between the lamps.
- The current is shared between the loops of the circuit.
- The current is the same at all points in the circuit.

Make a table and put each statement in the correct column.

Series circuits	Parallel circuits

2. You have two lamps and three switches. You want to make a parallel circuit that will:

- switch off both lamps together

and also:

- switch off each lamp separately.

Draw the circuit that will do this.

For your notes

You can connect lamps in **series** and in **parallel**. Parallel circuits have more than one loop.

Lamps in parallel are brighter than the same lamps in series, using the same battery.

In a series circuit:

- the current is the same at all points
- the voltage is shared between the lamps.

In a parallel circuit:

- the current is shared between the loops
- the voltage is the same across the battery and each lamp.

Magnets

Magnetic fields

You have probably discovered how a bar magnet acts when you put it near iron. A coil of wire with electricity passing through it acts like a magnet.

If you sprinkle iron filings around a magnet, you can see a pattern around the magnet. Iron filings are tiny pieces of iron. The magnet pulls the tiny pieces of iron towards it. We say the magnet has a **magnetic field**. Only iron filings inside the magnetic field are pulled. Photo **A** shows the field around a bar magnet. Photo **B** shows the field around a coil.

Both the bar magnet and the coil pull the iron filings into lines. We can show the lines by drawing **magnetic field lines**.

Magnetic field lines run from the **north pole** of the magnet to the **south pole** of the magnet. You can show the direction of the magnetic field lines using a compass.

Learn about

➤ Making magnets using electricity

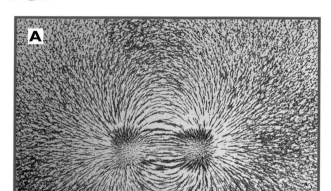

A

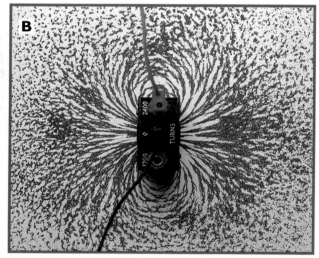

B

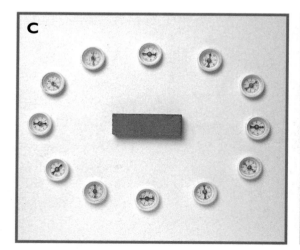

C

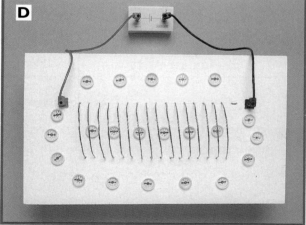

D

ⓐ Look at photo **D**. What do you think would happen if the current in the coil was turned off?

Magnets attract and repel

Two magnetic north poles push apart or **repel**. Two south poles repel. A north pole and a south pole pull together or **attract**. This is true of ordinary magnets (photo **E**) and the coil with the current (photo **F**).

b In photo **E**, the two magnets are pulling together. Draw a diagram showing the poles of the two magnets.

c Look at photo **F**. The two coils are pulling together. What would happen if the current was switched off?

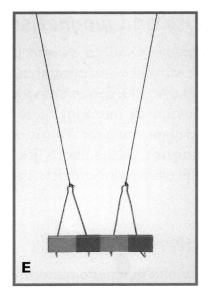

E

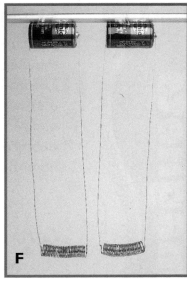

F

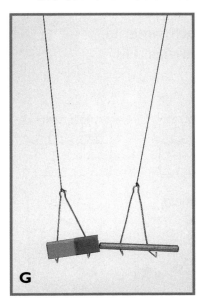

G

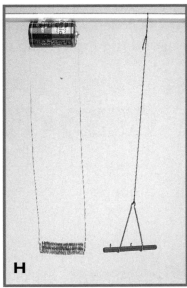

H

Magnetic materials

Magnets attract **magnetic materials**. Iron, nickel and cobalt are magnetic. Many metals contain some iron, nickel or cobalt so many metals are magnetic.

d Name three metals that will be attracted to a magnet.

e Name two metals that will not be attracted to a magnet.

The magnet and the coil attract a piece of iron.

Questions

1. What do we call:
   a the space around a magnet where iron filings are pulled?
   b the lines iron filings make near a magnet?
   c materials that are attracted to a magnet?
   d pushing apart?
   e pulling together?

2. A coil of wire connected to a battery behaves like a magnet. Give three ways the coil is like an ordinary magnet.

For your notes

A coil of wire connected to a battery makes a magnet.

Magnets make **magnetic fields**. Magnetic fields have **magnetic field lines**.

Like magnetic poles **repel**. Unlike poles **attract**.

Iron, nickel and cobalt are **magnetic** metals.

Electromagnets

Electricity and magnetism

You can connect a coil to a battery so that the electric current runs through it. The coil behaves like a weak magnet. Putting a **core** of magnetic material inside the coil makes a stronger magnet. This is called an **electromagnet**. In the photo you can see how the electromagnet attracts the keys.

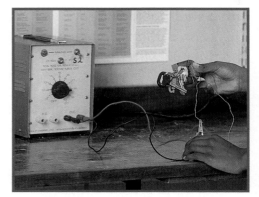

Core material

You can use any magnetic material for the core.

Craig carried out an investigation with electromagnets. He used different materials for the core. He coiled wire around each material, connected the wire to a battery and tried to pick up paperclips. His results are shown below.

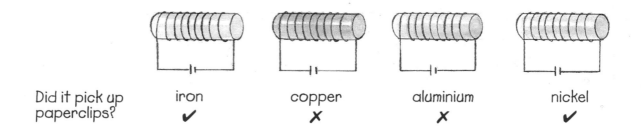

Did it pick up paperclips?	iron	copper	aluminium	nickel
	✔	✘	✘	✔

a Which metals are magnetic?

Most electromagnets have an iron core. Iron is only magnetic when it is in a magnetic field. Steel is different. Steel stays magnetic after it is removed from the magnetic field.

b Which material can be used to make a magnet you can turn off?

Stronger electromagnets: more batteries

Ruksham and Hannah wanted to make their electromagnet stronger. They increased the current by adding more batteries. They kept the same iron core and the same number of turns in the coil. The table shows their results.

Number of batteries	1	2	3	4	5
Current in A	0.2	0.4	0.6	0.8	1.0
Paperclips lifted	5	11	16	24	29

c What do the results show?

Stronger electromagnets: more turns

Gina and Scott also wanted to make their electromagnet stronger. They increased the number of turns in the coil. The table shows their results.

Number of turns	10	20	30	40	50
Current in A	0.5	0.5	0.5	0.5	0.5
Paperclips lifted	3	9	16	31	40

d Gina and Scott made an electromagnet with 25 turns. Predict how many paperclips it will lift.

> **To make a strong electromagnet you need to:**
> - **have an iron core**
> - **increase the current**
> - **have lots of turns in the coil.**

Using electromagnets

Huge electromagnets are used in scrap yards to pick up cars.

e Most cars are made of iron. Some modern cars are made of aluminium. What problem will this cause for scrap yard owners?

Questions

1. Terry is making an electromagnet. He is using an iron core. List two ways he can make his electromagnet stronger.

2. Electromagnets are used in scrap yards. Why would the electromagnet be made with an iron core rather than a steel core?

3. Plot a line graph of Ruksham and Hannah's results. Put current along the bottom and paperclips lifted up the side. Draw a line of best fit using a ruler.

For your notes

An **electromagnet** is a coil of wire with an electric current running through it and a **core** inside.

Electromagnets are made with an iron core so that they can be switched off.

Increasing the current in the coil makes an electromagnet stronger.

Increasing the number of turns in the coil of an electromagnet also makes it stronger.

The history of microscopes

Small is beautiful

Before scientists had microscopes, they could not see things that are very small. They could only guess what things looked like.

In 1670 a Dutchman called Antoni van Leeuwenhoek made a simple microscope with one lens. He used this microscope to study small objects. His microscope was very popular. Scientists everywhere began to use microscopes like it.

a Why do you think scientists liked this microscope?

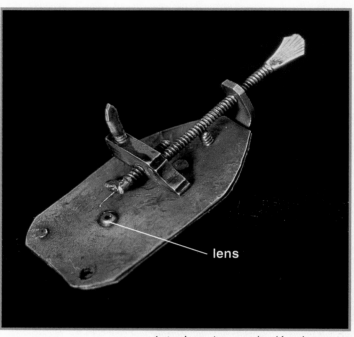

Antoni van Leeuwenhoek's microscope.

eyepiece lens

focus

objective lens

stage: the slide sits on here

mirror: sends the light up through the slide

condenser: controls how much light goes up through the slide

base

The compound microscope

A few years later, a British scientist called Robert Hooke changed the microscope. He added another lens to make objects look even bigger. This was called a **compound microscope**. Using this microscope, Hooke saw tiny compartments in a piece of cork. He thought they looked like tiny rooms and called them **cells**. The photo opposite shows a modern compound microscope.

b Name the two lenses in a compound microscope.

What can you see through a microscope?

A microscope shows that your skin is made of cells.

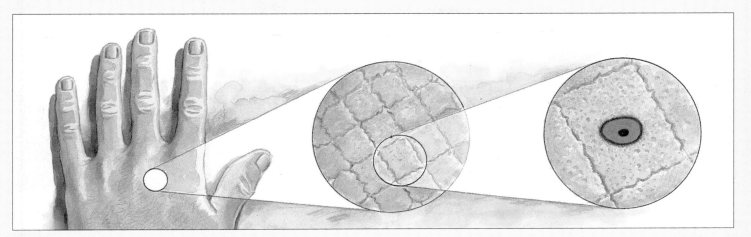

What you can see depends on how big the microscope can make things. We call this **magnification**. The objective lens can be changed to give different magnifications. To work out the total magnification, you multiply the power of the eyepiece lens by the power of the objective lens.

c What is the total magnification in a microscope that has an eyepiece lens of ×10 and an objective lens of ×4?

The electron microscope

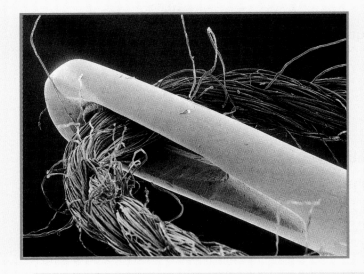

In 1932, a German engineer called Ernst Ruska built the first **electron microscope**. This showed a much more detailed picture than a compound microscope. A TV screen shows the image. The photo shows a needle and thread seen through an electron microscope.

The first electron microscope could only make things 40 times bigger. Modern ones can make things look 500 000 times bigger! Scientists have found out more about cells using these microscopes.

Questions

1. Write out each part of the microscope along with its correct job.

Microscope parts	Jobs
stage	focuses the image
lens	sends light up through the slide
condenser	holds the slide
mirror	controls the amount of light

2. Draw a time line to show the development of the microscope.

3. Imagine you are Robert Hooke. Write a letter to a friend explaining why your microscope is so important to scientists.

Building blocks

Types of cell

We are going to look more closely at cells. Scientists have discovered what cells look like inside using the electron microscope.

The house in the photo is built from thousands of bricks. All living things are also made up of tiny building blocks, called **cells**. A cell is so small that we can only see it with a microscope.

There are two main types of cell: **animal cells** and **plant cells**. They have a lot in common, but they also have some differences.

Learn about

► Animal cells

► Plant cells

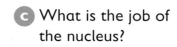

Animal cells

An animal cell is shown opposite. Around the outside of it is a thin **cell membrane**. The membrane lets substances in and out of the cell.

Inside the cell is a jelly-like liquid called **cytoplasm**. Chemical changes take place here.

Every cell has a **nucleus**. This controls everything that happens inside the cell.

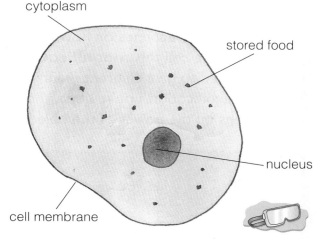

cytoplasm

stored food

nucleus

cell membrane

a What is the job of the cell membrane?

b What is the name of the liquid inside the cell?

c What is the job of the nucleus?

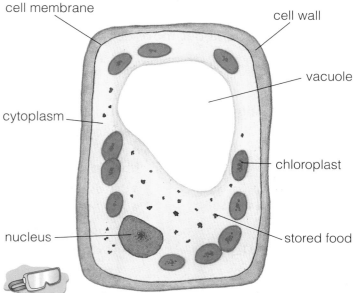

cell membrane

cell wall

vacuole

chloroplast

cytoplasm

nucleus

stored food

Plant cells

A plant cell is shown on the left. It has a cell membrane, a nucleus and cytoplasm, just as animal cells do.

Plant cells also have some parts that animal cells don't have.

Plant cells have lots of small structures called **chloroplasts**. These contain a green substance called **chlorophyll**. This is why plants look green. Plants make their food in these chloroplasts.

Every plant cell has a **cell wall** made of a strong substance called **cellulose**. This supports the cell and makes it strong. The photo below shows cellulose seen with an electron microscope.

Inside the cell is a **vacuole**. This contains a liquid called sap that keeps the cell firm.

d What is the cell wall made from?

e What is the green substance inside chloroplasts?

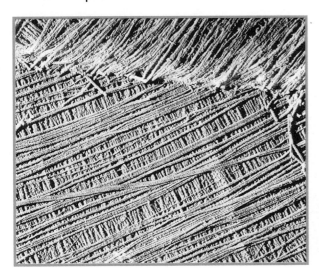

Cell shapes

Photo **A** shows human cheek cells (animal cells).
Photo **B** shows onion cells (plant cells).

Look at the difference in shape. Animal cells have an **irregular shape**. Plant cells have a **regular shape**.

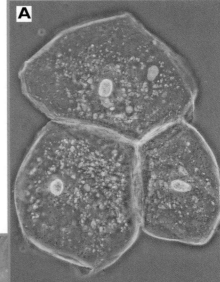

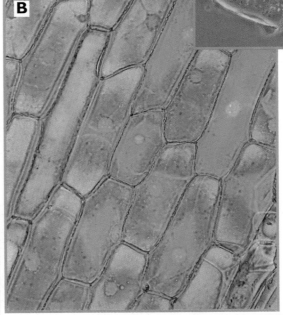

Questions

1. For each of these parts, write 'P' if a plant cell has it. Write 'A' if an animal cell has it.

     a cell membrane   **b** cell wall

     c cytoplasm   **d** nucleus

     e chloroplasts   **f** vacuole

2. What part of the cell does each job below?

     a controls the cell

     b gives the cell shape

     c lets substances in and out of the cell

     d place where chemical changes happen

For your notes

All living things are made of **cells**.

There are two types of cell: **animal cells** and **plant cells**.

Both types of cell have a **cell membrane**, **cytoplasm** and a **nucleus**.

Plant cells also have a **regular shape**, a **cell wall**, **chloroplasts** and a **vacuole**.

Photosynthesis

Making food

> **a** Plants do not eat food, so where do they get their food?

The photo shows a plant in the jungle.

> **b** What do you think the plant needs so it can grow?

I love the Sun

Plants make their own food in their leaves. This is called **photosynthesis**. It happens in the chloroplasts, which are mainly in leaf cells.

Plants take in carbon dioxide from the air and water from the soil. In photosynthesis, they use light energy from the Sun to turn these substances into sugars. Plants also make oxygen during photosynthesis.

Chloroplasts contain a green substance called **chlorophyll**. Chlorophyll absorbs light energy which is needed for photosynthesis. Look at the diagram below which shows what happens.

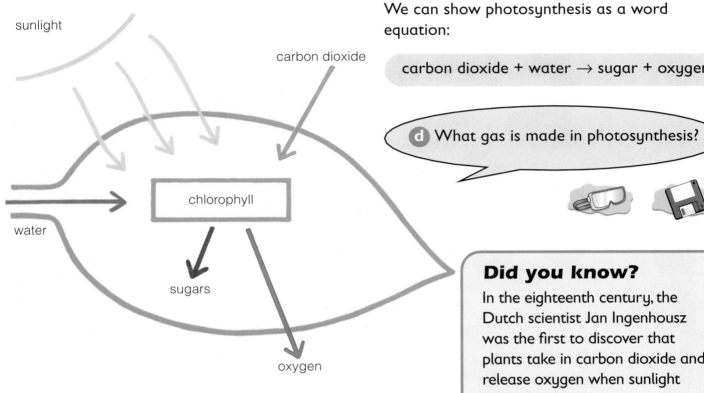

sunlight

carbon dioxide

chlorophyll

water

sugars

oxygen

c Why are most plants green?

We can show photosynthesis as a word equation:

carbon dioxide + water → sugar + oxygen

d What gas is made in photosynthesis?

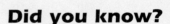

Did you know?

In the eighteenth century, the Dutch scientist Jan Ingenhousz was the first to discover that plants take in carbon dioxide and release oxygen when sunlight shines on them.

Questions

1. Copy and complete these sentences.

Photosynthesis uses _____ and _____ to make sugars.

The green substance in plants is called _____.

The gas made in photosynthesis is _____.

2. a What would happen to photosynthesis if a plant was kept in the dark for a few days?

b What would happen to photosynthesis if a plant was kept without any carbon dioxide?

3. Copy and complete the equation for photosynthesis.

carbon dioxide + _____ → sugar + _____

For your notes

Plants make food by a process called **photosynthesis**.

In photosynthesis, plants use light energy, carbon dioxide and water to make sugars and oxygen.

Leaves are food factories

a Look at the photo below and say what these leaves have in common.

Most leaves are broad and flat. They have a large surface so that they can trap as much sunlight as possible. Most leaves are green, because they contain chlorophyll.

b What are the three things plants need to make their food?

Did you know?
Some plants can move their leaves so that they face the Sun all day.

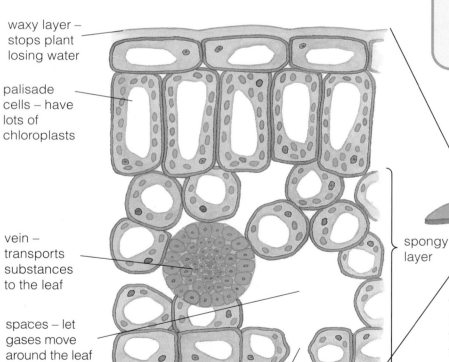

waxy layer – stops plant losing water

palisade cells – have lots of chloroplasts

vein – transports substances to the leaf

spaces – let gases move around the leaf

hole – lets gases in and out

spongy layer

The diagram on the left shows a slice through a leaf as seen through a microscope.

Plants need carbon dioxide, water and light energy to make their food. The diagram above shows the parts of the leaf and the jobs they do in photosynthesis.

c Look carefully at the diagram. List the parts that help the leaf get the carbon dioxide, water and light energy it needs.

Getting gases in and out

The diagram opposite shows a hole in the underside of a leaf. These holes are called **stomata**. The carbon dioxide needed for photosynthesis gets into the leaves through the stomata. The oxygen made during photosynthesis moves through the spaces and out of the leaf through the stomata.

Trapping light energy

The **palisade cell** is where most of the food is made. Palisade cells have lots of chloroplasts containing chlorophyll, so they can trap a lot of light energy. Palisade cells are close to the top surface of the leaf so that they get plenty of sunlight. The photo shows a palisade cell seen under a microscope.

carbon dioxide in   oxygen out from
for photosynthesis   photosynthesis

d Why do you think the palisade cells are at the top of a leaf, and not at the bottom?

e What do these cells have a lot of so that they can carry out photosynthesis?

Questions

1. Copy and complete these sentences.

All plants need _____ , _____ and light energy to make their food. Inside the palisade cells are parts called _____ . These contain a green substance called _____ .

2. Write out each part of the leaf along with its correct job.

Parts of leaf	Jobs
waxy layer	carries substances to the leaf
palisade cell	let gases into and out of the leaf
stomata	photosynthesis happens here
vein	stops the leaf losing water

3. a Which gas does the plant need for photosynthesis?

b Which gas does the plant make during photosynthesis?

4. How do gases get in and out of the leaf?

For your notes

The plant makes its food by photosynthesis in the leaves.

Leaves have a large surface to trap as much sunlight as possible.

Leaves have **stomata** so gases can move in and out.

85

The root of the problem

Plants need water

Plants need water to carry out photosynthesis. Water is carried into the leaves. Once the leaves have made food, water carries the food to where it is needed in the plant. Plants also need water to keep the cells firm and keep the plant upright.

How plants get their water

a Look at the photo below. Why do you think the roots grow so deep in the soil?

Learn about

► The job roots do

► Root hairs

Did you know?

Some parts of plants are almost all water. A ripe tomato is about 95% water.

The roots of a plant can become very large as they grow to reach water. The root has two main jobs:

- taking in water
- holding the plant firm in the soil.

Roots get thinner and thinner as they spread out. The very tips of roots have many tiny parts called **root hairs**. Root hairs are long and thin. They have a large surface to absorb water from the soil.

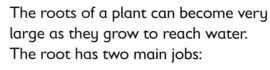

water

root hair

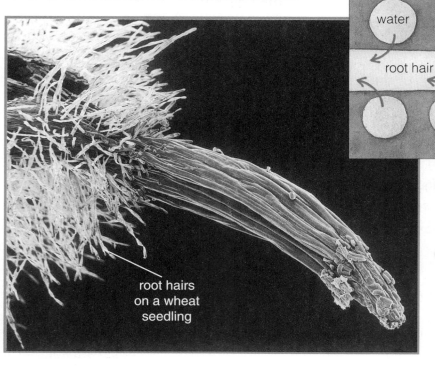

root hairs on a wheat seedling

b What are the two main jobs of roots?

c Describe what root hairs look like.

Getting water to all the parts of the plant

Water is transported through **veins** from the roots, up the stem to the leaves. Water is used in the leaves for photosynthesis. The food made in the leaves is then carried through the veins to other parts of the plant.

d What is the job of the plant's veins?

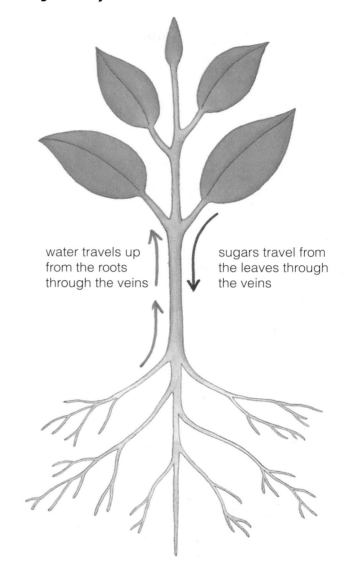

water travels up from the roots through the veins

sugars travel from the leaves through the veins

Did you know?
Florists stand white flowers in water with dye added. The dye travels up the veins and colours the flowers.

Questions

1. Copy and complete these sentences.

The roots take _____ into the plant. Roots are also important because they _____ plants in the soil. The ends of the roots have very tiny structures called _____ _____ . Water passes up the plant through the _____ .

2. Give three reasons why plants need water.

3. Write a story about how a water droplet travels through a plant, starting from the roots.

For your notes

The roots of a plant hold it firm in the ground, and absorb water.

Root hairs are tiny parts with a large surface to absorb water.

Water is transported around the plant through the **veins**.

Plant reproduction

Flowers

Flowers give great pleasure to people. William Wordsworth wrote a poem about their beauty.

> I wandered lonely as a cloud
> That floats on high o'er vales and hills
> When all at once I saw a crowd,
> A host of golden daffodils.

But this is not the reason why flowers exist.

a Why do you think a plant produces flowers?

Flowering plants reproduce by making seeds in the flowers. The seeds grow into new plants. The male parts of a flower are the **stamens**. Each stamen is made of an **anther** and a **filament**. The female parts are the **carpels**. Each carpel is made of a **stigma**, a **style** and an **ovary**.

b What are the stamens?

c Name the three parts of the carpel.

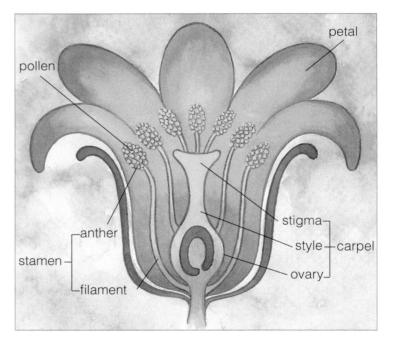

The male and female sex cells are found in flowers. The male sex cells are the **pollen grains**. Some pollen grains are shown in the photo. The female sex cell is the **egg cell**. Some flowers have just male sex cells, others have just female sex cells. Most flowers have both.

d Name the male and female sex cells in plants.

Pollination

Pollination happens when pollen grains move from an anther to a stigma. It may happen when pollen sticks to a bee and gets carried from one flower to the next. Pollination can also happen when wind blows pollen about.

Fertilisation

Fertilisation happens when the nucleus of the male sex cell joins with the nucleus of the female sex cell. In plants, fertilisation happens after pollination. The nucleus of the pollen grain joins with the nucleus of the egg cell, as shown opposite. This produces a fertilised egg cell.

 e What is fertilisation?

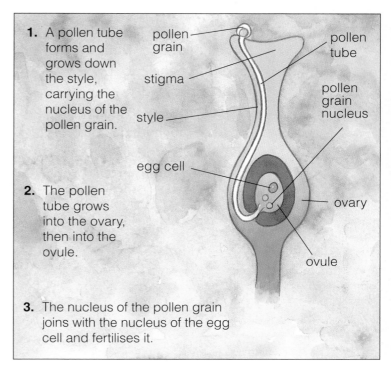

1. A pollen tube forms and grows down the style, carrying the nucleus of the pollen grain.

2. The pollen tube grows into the ovary, then into the ovule.

3. The nucleus of the pollen grain joins with the nucleus of the egg cell and fertilises it.

What happens to the fertilised egg cell?

The new fertilised egg cell grows to form an **embryo plant**. The ovule forms a **seed** with the embryo plant inside it. The seed protects the embryo plant and contains a food store for the tiny plant. The ovary forms the **fruit** with the seed inside it.

Questions

1. Write out each part of a flower along with its correct job.

Flower parts	Jobs
stigma	receives the pollen grains
carpel	male part of a flower
anther	female part of a flower
stamen	makes the pollen grains

2. Describe how a bee, called Polly Nation, helps with pollination.

3. Copy and complete this paragraph.

   In pollination, pollen grains transfer from the _____ to the _____ . Fertilisation happens when the nucleus of the _____ _____ joins with the nucleus of the _____ _____ . The fertilised cell forms an _____ _____ which is a tiny new plant inside the seed.

For your notes

Flowers contain the sex parts of the plant.

The male sex cells are the **pollen grains**.

The female sex cells are the **egg cells**.

Pollination is the transfer of the pollen grains from the **anther** to the **stigma**.

Fertilisation happens when the nucleus of the pollen grain joins with the nucleus of an egg cell.

Scaling up and down

Too small to see

A cell is smaller than the end of a pencil, so it is impossible to draw a cell at its real size. We need to draw it much larger than it really is. Scientists call this a **scale diagram**.

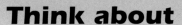

SOUTHEND-ON-SEA

Scale diagrams are also useful for showing things that are too big to fit on a page. We draw big things smaller than they really are. Maps are scale diagrams.

a Discuss in your group other uses for scale diagrams.

Scales

Scaling up means showing an object bigger than it really is. **Scaling down** means showing an object smaller than it really is.

The picture shows Mr and Mrs Beetroot with their two children Nick and Aileen. They are not

Mr Beetroot   Mrs Beetroot   Nick   Aileen

really this small. They have been scaled down. To find out how big they really are, we have to scale up again.

In this picture, 1 cm is used to show 40 cm in real life. In the picture Mr Beetroot is 5 cm tall. To find his real height you multiply his height in the picture by 40. This means you scale up by 40.

$5 \times 40 = 200$ So Mr Beetroot is 200 cm tall.

Instead of using lots of words to describe scaling up, we can say the **scale factor** for the picture is 40. This means you multiply by 40. So 1 cm represents 40 cm.

b Copy and complete the table to find the real heights of the rest of the Beetroot family.

Name	Picture height in cm	Scale factor	Picture height × scale factor	Real height in cm
Mr Beetroot	5	40	5 × 40	200
Mrs Beetroot	4	40		
Nick	3	40		
Aileen	2	40		

When we want to scale up, we multiply by a scale factor. Now imagine we want to scale down.

c Discuss in your group how you think we can scale down using the scale factor.

If you want to draw Mr Beetroot scaled down by a scale factor of 20, you divide his real height by 20.

200 ÷ 20 = 10 cm   So you would draw Mr Beetroot 10 cm tall.

d Draw a table with these headings and work out how big you would draw the rest of the Beetroot family.

Name	Real height in cm	Scale factor	Real height ÷ scale factor	Picture height in cm
Mr Beetroot	200	20	200 ÷ 20	10

Questions

1. The following table lists some of the objects in the Beetroots' house. Copy and complete the table.

Object	Real measurement in cm	Picture measurement in cm	Scale factor
Length of car		10	30
Height of car	150		30
Length of pencil		2	10
Height of bicycle	80		20

2. Measure your height in centimetres. Work out how you could draw a scale diagram to represent your height. Draw a line to show your height scaled down by a factor of 10.

Metals through the ages

Historic metals

Metals are very important in our lives. They were also very important in the lives of people throughout history.

The pictures below show the metals people have used over the last 7000 years. People use different metals for different things.

Look at the pictures.

a Which four metals did the ancient Egyptians use?

b Which people first started to use iron to make weapons?

c Which people invented cast iron in 300 BC?

d Who invented a way of making large amounts of cheap steel?

Before 5000 BC

Stone Age people found pieces of gold in rivers.

3000 BC

Egyptians used gold, silver, copper and bronze.

1200 BC

Hittites made wrought iron from rocks.

500 BC

Small pieces of steel were made from wrought iron.

300 BC

The Chinese invented cast iron. It was not used in Europe for 1100 years.

1665 AD

Dud Dudley started to make cast iron using coke instead of charcoal.

1856 AD

Henry Bessemer made large amounts of cheap steel.

Using metals

Gold and silver are used for jewellery. Steel is used to make bridges and large buildings. How a metal is used depends on:

● how it behaves. We call this the metal's **properties**.

● how easy it is to make.

On the next page are fact files for six historic metals.

> **Did you know?**
> In 688 AD the Chinese built a pagoda of cast iron that was 90 m tall.

Fact files

Gold
- yellow, very soft, very bendy
- found as gold, so very easy to use
- very rare

Copper
- pink, soft, flexible
- found as a rock and changed into copper (by heating with carbon)
- more common than gold

Cast iron (iron with lots of carbon)
- grey, hard, breaks when bent
- found as a rock
- the rock is heated with carbon to a very high temperature

Bronze (copper and tin mixture)
- brown, hard, breaks when bent
- copper and tin are found as rocks and are changed into metals
- the metals are melted together and mixed

Wrought iron (iron with almost no carbon)
- grey, soft, bendy
- found as a rock
- the rock is heated with carbon, then beaten with a hammer

Steel (iron with a little carbon)
- grey, hard, bends without breaking
- found as a rock
- made from cast iron by heating again and burning off some of the carbon

Look at the fact files.

e Which metal is found as a metal and not as a rock?

f Bronze is a mixture of copper and tin. How does copper change when it is made into bronze?

g Which type of iron is hard and does not break when bent?

h How do you make steel from rock?

Questions

1. A knife needs to be made of a hard metal so it will keep a sharp edge. It should not break when bent. Copy these sentences, choosing from the words in bold.

When you bend steel it **does/does not** break. Bronze and cast iron **do/do not** break when bent. Steel is **harder/softer** than wrought iron and copper. Steel knives keep a **sharper/blunter** edge than wrought iron or copper knives. Steel knives **do/do not** break easily.

2. Look back at 1200 BC in the pictures. The Hittites were the first people to use iron for knives. Imagine you are a Hittite blacksmith. You have started to make iron knives, but your customers want to buy the bronze knives they are used to.

Write a story about how you persuade your customers to buy iron knives. Use the fact files for wrought iron and bronze to help you.

What is a metal?

Properties

The **properties** of a material show how it behaves. We discover the properties of a material by asking questions like 'Does electricity pass through it?' or 'What temperature does it melt at?'. We are going to study the properties of metals.

Metals conduct electricity

You can use metals to complete a circuit because they let electricity pass through them. We say metals **conduct electricity**. Most wires are made of copper. The cables between electricity pylons are made of aluminium. The prongs on most plugs are made of brass. Brass is a mixture of copper and zinc.

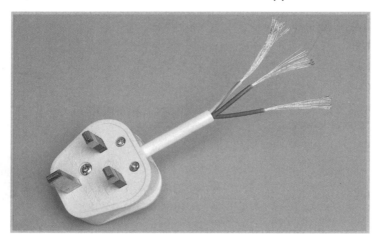

Metals conduct heat energy

We make saucepans of copper, cast iron, stainless steel and aluminium. Metals let heat energy pass easily. We say that metals **conduct heat energy**.

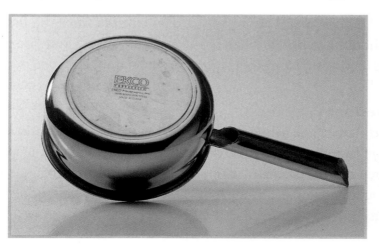

Learn about

▶ The properties of metals

Metals are shiny

Some metals are magnetic

Iron is **magnetic**, and so are nickel and cobalt. These metals are attracted to a magnet.

a Steel contains iron. How could you separate aluminium cans from steel cans?

Most metals are solids

We are comfortable living at 25 °C. Look at the chart opposite. The dotted line shows 25 °C.

b Which metal is a liquid at 25 °C? (Look along the dotted line.)

c Which other metal is a liquid at 100 °C?

d Which metal would melt when heated from 25 °C to 100 °C?

e Which metal is a solid even in the hottest part of a Bunsen burner flame?

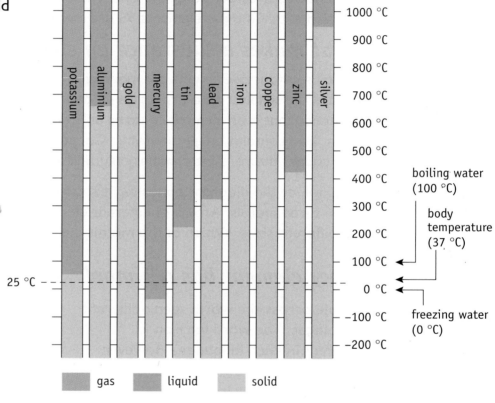

the hottest part of a Bunsen burner flame (1500 °C)

boiling water (100 °C)

body temperature (37 °C)

freezing water (0 °C)

gas   liquid   solid

Questions

1. Name a metal used in wires.
2. Name a metal used to make saucepans.
3. Name three metals that are magnetic.
4. Name two metals that are not magnetic.
5. Make a list of all the metals mentioned on these two pages. Add any other metals mentioned on pages 92–3. Put your list into alphabetical order. Which of these metals are mixtures of two substances?

For your notes

Metals are shiny.

Metals are good **conductors of electricity** and **heat energy**.

A few metals, including iron, are **magnetic**.

Most metals are solids at room temperature.

95

Elements

Some metals contain more than one substance. These metals are **mixtures**. Steel is a mixture of iron and carbon. Bronze is a mixture of copper and tin. Brass is a mixture of copper and zinc.

Metals that contain only one substance are **elements**. Gold, silver and copper are all elements. So are iron, nickel and zinc. There are 118 elements. Of these elements, 96 are metals.

What makes a substance an element?

Like all substances, elements are made up of particles. We call the simplest type of particle an **atom**. A substance that is an element contains only one type of atom. Iron contains only iron atoms. Copper contains only copper atoms. Zinc contains only zinc atoms.

a Look at the diagram opposite. It shows the atoms in three metals. Atoms of different elements are different sizes. Which of the metals are elements?

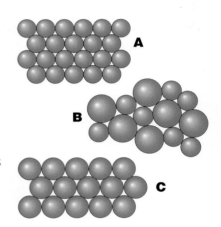

Every element has a symbol

People across the world speak different languages. The word for iron is different in each language. However, scientists across the world use the same **symbol** for iron. Each element has a symbol that scientists use.

b What is the symbol for iron?

c Imagine each symbol was one letter.

i How many different letters are there in the alphabet?

ii How many different symbols could there be?

iii How many elements are there?

iv Would there be enough symbols?

Some elements were chosen by people who spoke other languages. The symbol for iron, Fe, comes from the Latin word for iron (*ferrum*). Latin was the language spoken by the Romans. Silver has the symbol Ag, from the Latin word for silver (*argentum*). Tungsten has the symbol W, from the German word for tungsten (*wolfram*).

(d) Calcium, cobalt and copper are all elements starting with C. Which symbol below goes with which element? (Hint: the Latin name for copper was cuprum.)

Cu   Ca   Co

Putting the elements in order

Learning about the 118 elements takes a long time. We put the elements in a special table to make it easier. This table is called the **periodic table**. Most of the periodic table is shown below.

	metals
	non-metals

(e) Where are the metals in the periodic table? Are they to the left or to the right as you look at the table?

												H						0
I	II				←	Groups	→					III	IV	V	VI	VII	He	1
Li	Be											B	C	N	O	F	Ne	2
Na	Mg											Al	Si	P	S	Cl	Ar	3
K	Ca	Sc	Ti	V	Cr	Mn	Fe	Co	Ni	Cu	Zn	Ga	Ge	As	Se	Br	Kr	4
Rb	Sr	Y	Zr	Nb	Mo	Tc	Ru	Rh	Pd	Ag	Cd	In	Sn	Sb	Te	I	Xe	5
Cs	Ba	Lu	Hf	Ta	W	Re	Os	Ir	Pt	Au	Hg	Tl	Pb	Bi	Po	At	Rn	6
Fr	Ra	Lr	Rf	Db	Sg	Bh	Hs	Mt	Uun	Uuu	Uub	Uuq		Uuh		Uuo		7

Periods

The vertical columns in the periodic table are called **groups**. The elements in a group are alike. The horizontal rows are called **periods**.

Questions

1. Copy and complete this sentence.

   Elements are substances with …

2. Copper is an element. Brass is a mixture. Explain why copper is an element and why brass is not an element.

3. Lillian thinks that the element F is a metal. Sarah looks at the periodic table and says it is not a metal. Who is right? Why?

For your notes

We call the simplest type of particle an **atom**.

An **element** is a substance with only one type of atom.

Many metals are elements.

Each element has a **symbol**.

We arrange the elements in the **periodic table**.

The periodic table has **groups** (columns) and **periods** (rows).

Learn about

➤ Non-metals

Some more elements

We have seen that most metals are solids.
Metals are shiny, and they conduct electricity and heat energy.

Look at the fact files below.

a Do these elements:

    i look shiny?

    ii conduct electricity?

    iii conduct heat energy?

b Are these elements solids at room temperature?

c Are these elements metals?

d Look at the periodic table on page 97. Are these elements to the left or right of the table?

Fact files: some gases

Element: **Oxygen**

Symbol: O

State at 25 °C: gas

Colour: colourless

Conduct electricity? ✗

Conduct heat energy? ✗

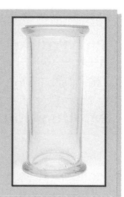

Element: **Chlorine**

Symbol: Cl

State at 25 °C: gas

Colour: green

Conduct electricity? ✗

Conduct heat energy? ✗

Element: **Nitrogen**

Symbol: N

State at 25 °C: gas

Colour: colourless

Conduct electricity? ✗

Conduct heat energy? ✗

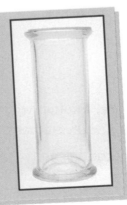

Element: **Helium**

Symbol: He

State at 25 °C: gas

Colour: colourless

Conduct electricity? ✗

Conduct thermal energy? ✗

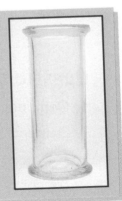

Fact files: a liquid and a solid

Element: Bromine

Symbol:	Br
State at 25 °C:	liquid
Colour:	red
Conduct electricity?	✗
Conduct heat energy?	✗

Element: Sulphur

Symbol:	S
State at 25 °C:	solid
Colour:	yellow
Conduct electricity?	✗
Conduct heat energy?	✗

Look at the fact file about bromine.

e Do you think that bromine is a metal?

f Give four reasons for your answer.

g Look back at the periodic table. Is bromine to the left or right of the table?

Look at the fact file about sulphur.

h Is sulphur a metal?

i Give three reasons for your answer.

Non-metal elements

The elements on these two pages are **non-metals**. Unlike metals, most non-metals are not shiny solids. They do not conduct electricity or heat energy very well. There are lots of non-metals with different properties. Some of them are solids, and some are liquids. Many of them are gases.

Some of these gases are very useful. Oxygen is used to keep sick babies alive. Chlorine is used to kill bacteria in drinking water. Helium is a gas that is lighter than air, so balloons filled with helium float.

Questions

1. Name a non-metal that is:

   a a liquid

   b a green gas

   c a yellow solid

   d a colourless gas that we need to live.

2. In what three ways are most non-metals different from most metals?

3. Neon is an element. It is a colourless gas. It does not conduct heat energy or electricity.

   a Is neon a metal or a non-metal?

   b Explain your answer.

For your notes

Some elements are **non-metals**.

Most non-metals are not shiny.

Most non-metals do not conduct electricity.

Most non-metals do not conduct heat energy.

Some non-metals are solids, some are liquids and some are gases at room temperature.

Getting it right

Metal or non-metal?

Scientists have used the properties of metals to decide that:

- aluminium, iron, copper, nickel and mercury are metals
- hydrogen, sulphur, bromine and chlorine are non-metals.

Joe's class want to put these nine elements into two groups, metals and non-metals. There are fact files for the nine elements on the opposite page.

Lillian's idea

Put all the solids in one group. Metals are solids. All the others will be non-metals.

a i Which elements will be in Lillian's 'metals' group?

ii Which elements will be in Lillian's 'non-metals' group?

iii Is Lillian's idea going to work? Explain your answer.

Joe's idea

Test the elements with a magnet. The ones that stick to the magnet are metals. The others are non-metals.

b i Which elements will be in Joe's 'metals' group?

ii Which elements will be in Joe's 'non-metals' group?

iii Is Joe's idea going to work? Explain your answer.

Yasmin's idea

See which elements conduct electricity. The ones that do are metals, the others are non-metals.

c i Which elements will be in Yasmin's 'metals' group?

ii Which elements will be in Yasmin's 'non-metals' group?

iii Is Yasmin's idea going to work? Explain your answer.

What about carbon?

Their teacher then gives them a piece of carbon. The table below shows some properties of carbon. Scientists say that carbon is a non-metal.

d Would: **i** Lillian **ii** Joe **iii** Yasmin say that carbon was a non-metal?

e Think of an idea that will work for all the elements shown, including carbon.

Element	State at 25°C	Colour	Shiny?	Magnetic?	Conduct electricity?	Conduct heat energy?
Carbon	Solid	Black	✗	✗	✔	✔

Fact files

The metals are in yellow boxes. The non-metals are in pink boxes.

Element: Copper

Symbol:	Cu
State at 25 °C:	solid
Colour:	pink
Shiny?	✔
Magnetic?	✘
Conduct electricity?	✔
Conduct heat energy?	✔

Element: Aluminium

Symbol:	Al
State at 25 °C:	solid
Colour:	silver
Shiny?	✔
Magnetic?	✘
Conduct electricity?	✔
Conduct heat energy?	✔

Element: Iron

Symbol:	Fe
State at 25 °C:	solid
Colour:	grey
Shiny?	✔
Magnetic?	✔
Conduct electricity?	✔
Conduct heat energy?	✔

Element: Nickel

Symbol:	Ni
State at 25 °C:	solid
Colour:	grey
Shiny?	✔
Magnetic?	✔
Conduct electricity?	✔
Conduct heat energy?	✔

Element: Mercury

Symbol:	Hg
State at 25 °C:	liquid
Colour:	silver
Shiny?	✔
Magnetic?	✘
Conduct electricity?	✔
Conduct heat energy?	✔

Element: Hydrogen

Symbol:	H
State at 25 °C:	gas
Colour:	colourless
Shiny?	✘
Magnetic?	✘
Conduct electricity?	✘
Conduct heat energy?	✘

Element: Sulphur

Symbol:	S
State at 25 °C:	solid
Colour:	yellow
Shiny?	✘
Magnetic?	✘
Conduct electricity?	✘
Conduct heat energy?	✘

Element: Bromine

Symbol:	Br
State at 25 °C:	liquid
Colour:	red
Shiny?	✘
Magnetic?	✘
Conduct electricity?	✘
Conduct heat energy?	✘

Element: Chlorine

Symbol:	Cl
State at 25 °C:	gas
Colour:	green
Shiny?	✘
Magnetic?	✘
Conduct electricity?	✘
Conduct heat energy?	✘

Questions

1. Carbon has two forms, graphite and diamond, shown in the table below.
Scientists say that carbon is a non-metal. Do you agree? Explain your answer.

	State at 25 °C	Colour	Shiny?	Magnetic?	Conduct electricity?	Conduct heat energy?
Graphite	Solid	**Black**	✘	✘	✔	✔
Diamond	Solid	**Colourless**	✘	✘	✘	✘

Heating metals

Melting and freezing

When you heat a metal, it melts. The solid becomes a liquid. When it cools, the liquid becomes a solid again. This is a **reversible** change. It is an example of a **physical change**. No new substances are made in a physical change.

Look at the table of melting points opposite.

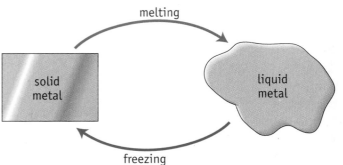

melting

solid metal

liquid metal

freezing

a Which metal is a liquid at room temperature (25 °C)?

b Which metal would melt if you heated it from 25 °C to body temperature (37 °C)?

c Which metal would melt if you heated it from 37 °C to 1000 °C using a Bunsen burner?

Metal	Melting point in °C
Cadmium	321
Mercury	−39
Gallium	30

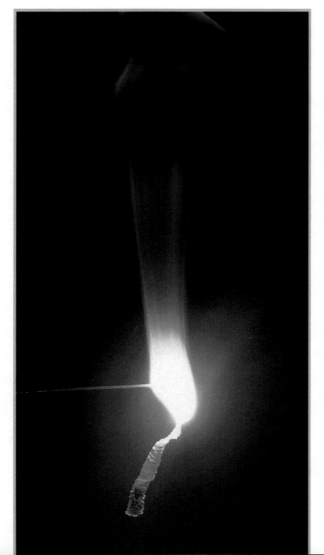

Making new substances

When you heat the metal magnesium in air, it burns. Light energy and heat energy are given out. The metal is burned and a white powder is made. The white powder does not turn back into magnesium as it cools. This is an **irreversible** change.

The magnesium has reacted with oxygen. This is a **chemical change** or **chemical reaction**. A new substance has been made. The new substance is called magnesium oxide.

d If Harry melts magnesium, what will he see?

e If Harry burns magnesium, what will he see?

f How is melting different from burning?

A different gas

When you burn a metal in air, you make a metal **oxide**. The metal magnesium reacts with oxygen in the air to make magnesium oxide.

> magnesium + oxygen → magnesium oxide

g Copy and complete this word equation for the reaction of the metal lithium with oxygen.

> lithium + oxygen → _____

What happens if we use a different gas instead of oxygen? If we use chlorine gas, we make a **chloride**. Sodium is a silver metal. Chlorine is a green gas. They react to make sodium chloride, a white powder. The photo opposite shows this.

> sodium + chlorine → sodium chloride

A different non-metal

Oxygen and chlorine are both non-metals. Metals will also react with other non-metals.

If we use sulphur instead of oxygen, we make a **sulphide**. Look at the photo opposite. When iron is heated with sulphur, it starts to glow. The chemical reaction gives out light energy and heat energy. Iron sulphide is made.

> iron + sulphur → iron sulphide

Questions

1. Physical changes can be reversed. Study the list of changes below. List the ones that are physical changes.

> **melting ice   a match burning   baking a cake
> boiling water   dissolving sugar   iron rusting**

2. Copy and complete the word equations.
   a magnesium + _____ → magnesium oxide
   b aluminium + oxygen → _____
   c sodium + _____ → sodium chloride
   d potassium + chlorine → _____

3. Write a word equation for the reaction between potassium and oxygen.

For your notes

No new substances are made during a **physical change**. New substances are made in a **chemical reaction**.

An **oxide** is made when a metal reacts with oxygen.

A **chloride** is made when a metal reacts with chlorine.

A **sulphide** is made when a metal reacts with sulphur.

Rusting

Building bridges

When we leave iron outside, it changes. The metal turns into the brown substance that we call **rust**. Scientists call rust **iron oxide**.

We build bridges of iron because it is strong. A bridge of rust would break easily. The bridge would have to be rebuilt. We need to stop the iron rusting, so we don't need to replace it.

a Iron changes when it rusts. What does the iron turn into?

Rusting is one type of **corrosion**. Many metals corrode, but only iron rusts.

Learn about

▶ Rusting

What makes iron rust?

A scientist took pieces of iron and put them in jars. The gas inside each jar was different. The jars were sealed. The results are shown in the diagram.

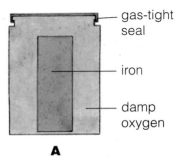

gas-tight seal — iron — damp oxygen

A

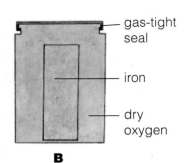

gas-tight seal — iron — dry oxygen

B

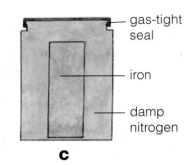

gas-tight seal — iron — damp nitrogen

C

b Which piece of iron went rusty?

c Which jars contained oxygen?

d Which jars contained water?

e Which jar contained both oxygen and water?

f What three substances have to be present for rusting to happen?

Preventing rusting

Oxygen and water must both be present for iron to rust. If the oxygen and water cannot get to the iron, it will not rust.

g Painting an iron bridge stops it rusting. Explain why.

Coating iron with tin stops it rusting. Tin does not rust as iron does. The layer of tin keeps the oxygen and water away from the iron.

h Explain why coating an iron bucket with tin will stop it rusting.

Steel is mostly iron, so it rusts. **Stainless steel** does not rust. Stainless steel contains chromium. The chromium forms a layer of chromium oxide on the surface of the steel. This layer stops the oxygen and water reaching the iron.

i Explain why stainless steel cutlery does not rust.

Questions

1. Is rusting a reversible change or an irreversible change?

2. Is rusting a physical change or a chemical reaction?

3. Study the experiment shown opposite. Say whether each nail will rust. Give reasons for your answers.

4. How would you stop an iron bridge from rusting?

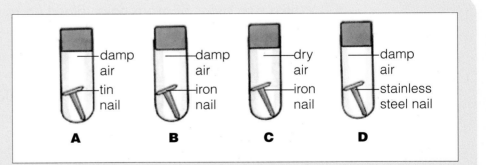

A — damp air, tin nail
B — damp air, iron nail
C — dry air, iron nail
D — damp air, stainless steel nail

For your notes

Iron **rusts** when oxygen and water can get to it.

Rusting turns iron into **iron oxide**.

Rusting is one type of **corrosion**. Corrosion destroys metals.

Compounds

Joining up

Magnesium oxide is not a metal or a non-metal. Magnesium oxide is not an element. It does not have a place in the periodic table.

Magnesium oxide is made when magnesium and oxygen react together. Magnesium oxide contains both magnesium atoms and oxygen atoms. The magnesium atoms and the oxygen atoms have joined up. Substances with more than one type of atom joined up are called **compounds**.

Learn about

➤ Compounds

magnesium   +   oxygen   ⟶   magnesium oxide

(a) Which two types of atom have joined up to make magnesium oxide?

Some compounds are solids

Magnesium oxide is a solid. The particles are close together and arranged in neat rows. When a metal reacts with a non-metal, you always get a solid compound.

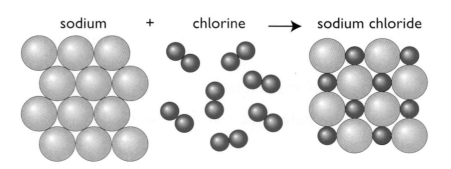

sodium   +   chlorine ⟶ sodium chloride

(b) Which two types of atom have joined up to make sodium chloride?

Some compounds are liquids or gases

Not all compounds are solids. Water is a compound. Water contains hydrogen and oxygen atoms joined together. Water is a liquid at room temperature.

Carbon dioxide is also a compound. Carbon dioxide contains carbon and oxygen atoms joined together. Carbon dioxide is a gas at room temperature.

c What two types of atom have joined up to make water?

d What two types of atom have joined up to make carbon dioxide?

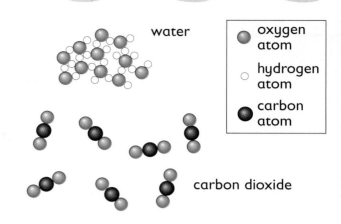

water

- oxygen atom
- hydrogen atom
- carbon atom

carbon dioxide

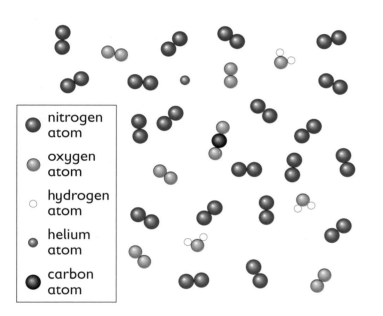

- nitrogen atom
- oxygen atom
- hydrogen atom
- helium atom
- carbon atom

Did you know?

The pictures of atoms on these pages are 25 million times bigger than the real atoms.

Mixtures, elements and compounds

The materials around us are usually **mixtures** of different substances. Steel is a mixture of two elements, iron and carbon. Sugar solution is a mixture of two compounds, water and sugar. A material that contains only one substance is **pure**. Pure iron contains only the element iron. Pure water contains only the compound water.

Air is a mixture. The diagram opposite shows the particles in air.

Questions

1. Copy and complete these sentences by choosing from the words in bold.

   a Elements contain **one type/more than one type** of atom.

   b Compounds contain **one type/more than one type** of atom joined together.

2. Study the diagram above showing the particles in air.

   a Draw the different substances in the air.

   b How many substances can you find that are elements?

   c Name the elements you find.

   d How many substances can you find that are compounds?

   e Name the compounds you find.

For your notes

A **compound** is a substance with more than one type of atom joined together.

A **pure** substance contains only one element or compound.

107

Forces everywhere

Everything you do uses forces. You cannot see forces, but you can often see the effects of a force. A force can change the shape of an object, or make it move faster or slower, or make it change direction. You can see the effects of forces in the sports day events happening on this page. 'Push' and 'pull' are two types of forces.

a What units do we use to measure forces?

Throwing

Look at Sam throwing the javelin. He runs and then throws the javelin to make it go as far as possible.

b What force does Sam use to make the javelin move, a push, a pull or both?

Running

In the race, Alex had to run hard against the strong wind. At the end of the race Alex was told how fast she ran.

c When Alex runs, what sort of force acts against her from the wind?

Jumping

James was in the pole-vault competition. He put the long pole in the ground and jumped up.

d What sort of force does James use on the pole?

After James had jumped he fell back onto the soft mat. Gravity pulled him down to the ground. Gravity is the force that pulls everything towards the centre of the Earth.

Sports day in Australia

The Earth is shaped like a ball. Britain and Australia are almost on opposite sides.

Gravity pulls the girls downwards.

e Which way is 'downwards' in Australia?

f Why does Shirley not fall off Australia?

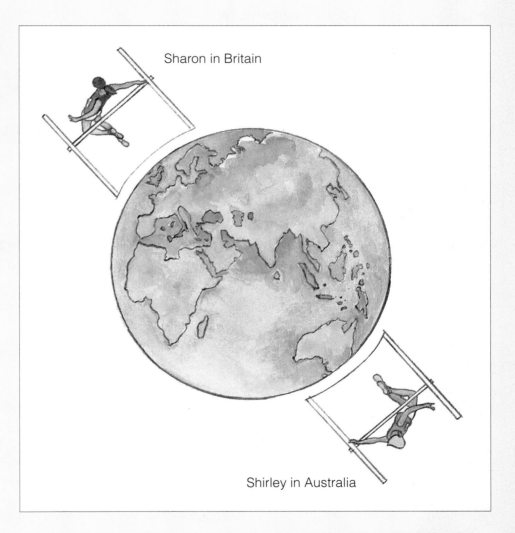

Sharon in Britain

Shirley in Australia

Questions

1. Copy and complete these sentences.

A force can change the _____ of an object.

A force can make something move _____ or _____.

2. Give three examples of how forces are useful in everyday life.

3. What is the name of the force that pulls you back to the ground when you jump?

Forces and gravity

What is weight?

Samson has to pull up against a force to pick up the dumbbell. This force is the dumbbell's **weight**, which pulls it down.

Weight is the force of gravity on an object. Heavy objects are pulled down with a bigger force than light objects. We measure weight in units called **newtons, N**.

a In which direction does the weight of the dumbbell act?

b Which of these weights will have the biggest pull?

> 10 N   20 N   100 N

Samson's pull

dumbbell's weight

What is gravity?

Gravity is the force that pulls everything towards the centre of the Earth. The Moon also has gravity pulling things towards its centre, but the Moon's gravity is weaker than the Earth's.

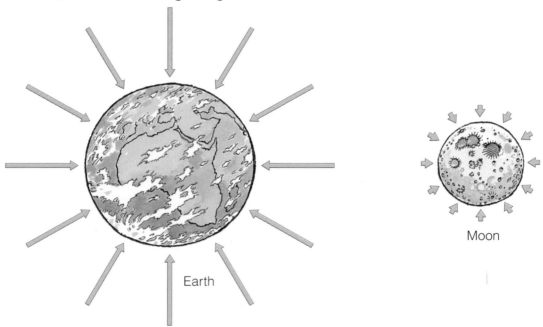

Earth

Moon

On Earth, Flo weighs about 660 N. On the Moon she weighs only 110 N. The Moon's gravity is one-sixth the strength of the Earth's gravity.

c Would you weigh more on the Earth or on the Moon?

d If you weighed 600 N on Earth, what would you weigh on the Moon?

Mass and weight

Imagine Flo goes to the Moon for lunar sports day. She is still the same size and shape as she is on Earth. She is still made of the same amount of stuff or matter. Flo's **mass** is a measure of how much matter she is made of. Mass is measured in **kilograms, kg**.

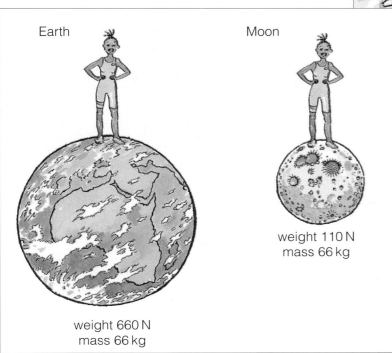

Earth

weight 660 N
mass 66 kg

Moon

weight 110 N
mass 66 kg

Flo's mass is the same on Earth and on the Moon. Her weight is different, because her weight is the force of gravity pulling on her mass. To find the weight of something on Earth you multiply its mass by 10.

e If Simon's mass is 55 kg, what is his weight on Earth?

Questions

1. Copy and complete these sentences.

   Weight is the force of _____ on an object. We measure weight in _____.

   Mass is a measure of how much _____ an object is made of. Mass is measured in _____.

   Your mass is the _____ on Earth and on the Moon but your _____ is different.

2. Calculate the weight on Earth of the people below:

   a Susan, mass 70 kg

   b Philippa, mass 55 kg

   c Marco, mass 88 kg.

3. What is gravity?

For your notes

Gravity is the force that pulls everything towards the centre of the Earth.

Weight is the force of gravity on an object. Weight is a force, measured in **newtons, N**.

Mass is a measure of how much matter an object is made of. Mass is measured in **kilograms, kg**.

111

Friction

What is friction?

Friction is a force that is made when things rub together. Friction can slow things down. The runner's shoes have good grip and make lots of friction with the ground to help her slow down. The duck's feet have very little friction with an icy lake, so it is difficult to stop.

a What kind of surfaces make the most friction?

b What kind of surfaces make the least friction?

Friction can be useful

Friction can be a very useful force. Bikes and cars have brakes that use friction to slow them down or stop them. The surfaces of the brakes rub against the wheels so the wheels don't turn so fast.

c Think of another example showing how friction is useful in everyday life.

Reducing friction

Sometimes friction is not useful and we want to reduce it. When two surfaces rub together, they will become worn down because of friction.

Machines have a lot of parts that rub together. To reduce friction, we use oil and grease. We call these **lubricants**. They make surfaces run smoothly against each other.

d What would you do to make the chain on your bike run smoothly?

Friction makes things warm

Where there is friction, heat energy is given out. You can feel this happen when you rub your hands together. They feel warm.

Air resistance

Air makes friction with moving objects such as cars and planes. We call this **air resistance**. It slows things down. Parachutists use air resistance to slow them down when they are falling towards the ground.

Racing cars move very fast. The one in the photo is shaped to keep air resistance low. We call this a **streamlined** shape.
The other car is not as streamlined and will have more air resistance.

If a car has too much air resistance, it will have a high **fuel consumption**. This means that it will use more litres of petrol for each kilometre it travels.

e Name three other things that are streamlined.

Questions

1. Copy and complete these sentences.

   Friction is made when two surfaces

   _____ _____.

   Where there is friction, _____ energy is given out.

   Friction can be reduced by using _____ such as oil and _____.

   When air causes friction, it is called

   _____ _____.

2. Write a story about a world without friction.

3. Draw a design for a car or speedboat that will have very little air resistance.

For your notes

Friction is a force that acts when things rub against each other.

Air resistance is a form of friction.

We can reduce or increase friction.

Unbalanced forces

Force arrows

The box in the picture opposite has two forces acting on it. One is the pull of the rope. The other is the weight of the box.

The diagram below shows these forces with **force arrows**. A force arrow points in the direction of the force. The length of the arrow shows the size of the force.

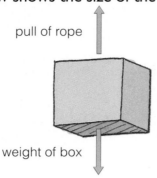

pull of rope

weight of box

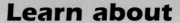
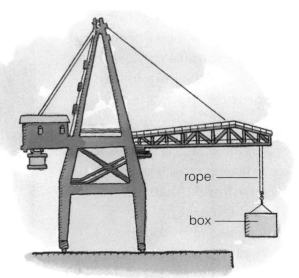

rope

box

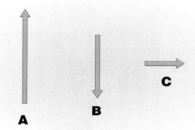

A

B

C

(a) Which of the arrows **A**, **B** and **C** shows the biggest force?

(b) Which one shows the smallest force?

(c) Which one could show someone's weight?

Getting going

If Dipal does not push his go-kart, it will not start moving.
A force is needed to start something moving.

Dipal gave his go-kart a gentle push. It did not move at all.

(d) What force do you think stopped the go-kart moving?

Dipal gave his go-kart a bigger push. Dipal's push on the go-kart was bigger than friction, so the go-kart started to move.

Dipal's push

friction

When forces push against each other like this, and one force is bigger than the other, they are called **unbalanced forces**.

> **When there are unbalanced forces acting on an object, the object starts to move. It moves in the direction of the bigger force and it gets faster.**

e What will happen to the boxes **D** and **E** below?

Unbalanced forces on moving objects

Unbalanced forces can act on something that is already moving. The car in the diagram is moving forwards.

Because the force from the engine is bigger than the air resistance, the car moves faster.

force of engine   air resistance

> **When the bigger force is in the same direction as the movement, the object speeds up.**
> **When the bigger force is in the opposite direction to the movement, the object slows down.**

Questions

1. Copy and complete these sentences.

   When there are unbalanced forces acting on an object, the object starts to _____. It moves in the direction of the _____ force and it gets faster.

   When the bigger force is in the same direction as the movement, the object moves _____.

   When the bigger force is in the opposite direction to the movement, the object moves _____.

2. Draw arrows to show the following forces. Use 1 cm to show 1 N. So you would draw an arrow 2 cm long to show a force of 2 N.

   a 1 N   **b** 5 N   **c** 10 N   **d** 4 N

For your notes

Unbalanced forces can act on an object that is not moving. The object starts to move in the direction of the bigger force.

Unbalanced forces can act on a moving object. If the bigger force is in the same direction as the movement, then the object moves faster. If the bigger force is in the opposite direction to the movement, then the object moves slower.

Balanced forces

Staying put

Unbalanced forces make things move. Sometimes forces can act on an object, but the object will stay where it is.

Look at the picture of the tug-of-war between Zena and Sam. They are not moving. They are pulling with the same sized force, but in opposite directions. If two forces are the same size and pull in opposite directions, the forces are **balanced**.

> Why might an object stay where it is even when there are forces acting on it?

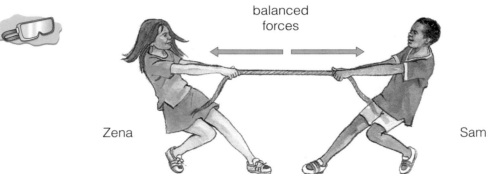

balanced forces

Zena

Sam

a Look at the diagrams below and decide which show balanced forces.

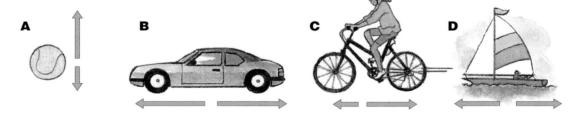

A   B   C   D

b For each object above, say whether it will move or stay still. If it will move, in which direction will it go?

Balanced forces

The picture opposite shows a weight hanging from a spring on a newtonmeter. The weight is not moving. The forces on it are balanced. The weight is pulling down on the spring with the same force as the spring pulls up on the weight.

The spring has stretched. The amount it stretches is called the **extension**. The extension depends on how much weight is hung on the spring.

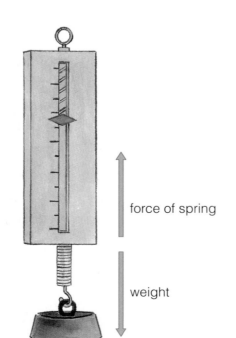

force of spring

weight

Mr Blue the decorator stands on a plank to paint a wall. He stands very still. The plank bends because of Mr Blue's weight. It pushes up. This force from the plank is called a **reaction force**. The force pushing down on the plank is the same as the force pushing up on Mr Blue. The forces are balanced.

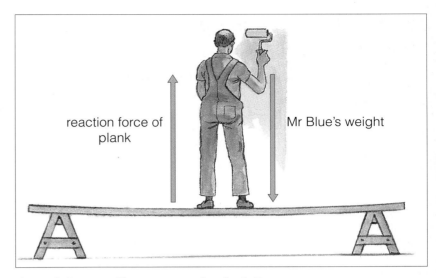

reaction force of plank

Mr Blue's weight

b What are the forces on your chair when you sit still on it? Draw a diagram with arrows.

Why do things float and sink?

When an object is put into water, the water pushes up on the object. This force is called **upthrust**. The object pushes down on the water. This force is called **weight**. If the object floats, then the upthrust is equal to the weight. The forces are balanced. If the object sinks, then the upthrust and weight are not equal. The forces are unbalanced.

There are also balanced forces when a hot-air balloon floats in air.

c What is the name of the force that pushes up on the balloon?

d What is the name of the force that pushes down on the air?

Questions

1. Copy and complete these sentences.

   When two forces are equal and in opposite directions, they are called _____ forces.

   If a man pulls a dog with a force of 10 N, and the dog pulls the man with a force of _____, the forces are balanced.

   The forces of _____ and _____ are balanced when a hot-air balloon floats.

2. Gianni pulled his dog with a force of 40 N and the dog pulled back against him with a force of 40 N. Draw a diagram of this and say why the forces are balanced.

3. Explain why a boat floats on water.

For your notes

If two forces are the same size and pull in opposite directions, they are called **balanced forces**.

The **reaction force** stops something falling through a solid object. The reaction force balances the weight.

When an object floats, the forces of **weight** and **upthrust** are equal.

117

Speed

Talking about speed

People use different sayings to describe how fast or slow things move.

As fast as the speed of light

As swift as a deer

Slower than a snail

Faster than a speeding bullet

We can tell how fast a thing moves by measuring its **speed**.

How do we measure speed?

To find the speed of an object, you need to know the distance the object travels and the time it takes to travel that distance. You take the distance travelled and divide by the time taken. We can show it like this:

$$\text{speed} = \frac{\text{distance travelled}}{\text{time taken}} \quad \begin{array}{l}\text{(in metres, m)}\\ \text{(in seconds, s)}\end{array}$$

Units of speed

We measure distance in metres or kilometres and time in seconds or hours. In science, we measure speed in metres per second, m/s. In everyday life, we find it easier to measure speed in kilometres per hour, km/h.

Example 1

A dog ran 30 metres in 2 seconds.

$$\text{dog's speed} = \frac{30 \text{ metres travelled}}{2 \text{ seconds taken}}$$

$$= \frac{30 \text{ m}}{2 \text{ s}} = 15 \text{ m/s}$$

The dog ran at a speed of 15 metres per second or 15 m/s. This means it ran 15 metres every second.

Example 2

In a sponsored walk at school, Danny walked 8 kilometres in 2 hours.

$$\text{Danny's speed} = \frac{8 \text{ kilometres travelled}}{2 \text{ hours taken}} = \frac{8 \text{ km}}{2 \text{ h}} = 4 \text{ km/h}$$

Danny walked at a speed of 4 kilometres per hour or 4 km/h. This means he walked 4 kilometres every hour.

a If Susan runs 100 metres in 20 seconds, what is her speed? Show how you worked it out.

How fast do things move?

The picture opposite shows the speeds of some moving objects.

b Which is the fastest animal?

c At what speed does it travel?

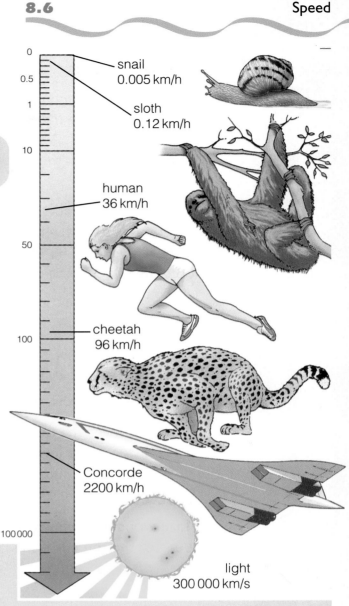

snail 0.005 km/h

sloth 0.12 km/h

human 36 km/h

cheetah 96 km/h

Concorde 2200 km/h

light 300 000 km/s

Questions

1. Copy and complete these sentences.

The speed of an object is usually measured in metres per _____ or _____ per hour.

To find the speed of an object, you must find the _____ the object travels and the time taken for it to travel that _____.

2. Copy the table below and fill in the correct figures for **A** to **D**.

Distance travelled	Time taken	Speed
100 km	2 hours	A
40 metres	8 seconds	B
200 km	4 hours	C
150 km	3 hours	D

For your notes

Speed is the distance an object travels in a certain time.

$$\text{speed} = \frac{\text{distance travelled (in metres)}}{\text{time taken (in seconds)}}$$

The units used for speed are metres per second, m/s, or kilometres per hour, km/h.

Forces and relationships

Variables

We link things together using **relationships**. In experiments we find the relationship between variables. A **variable** is the thing that we change or that is changed in an experiment.

In a javelin competition, the more force an athlete uses to throw the javelin, the further it will go. The variables are the force the athlete uses and the distance the javelin travels.

The relationship is:

- the more force the athlete uses, the greater the distance the javelin will travel.

We can also give the relationship as:

- the less force the athlete uses, the smaller the distance the javelin will travel.

Fast cars

Mary wondered what would happen to the speed of the toy car if she changed the slope.

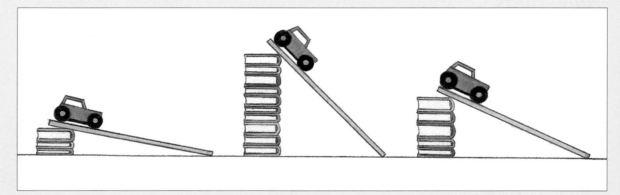

Discuss what you think would happen to the speed of Mary's car.

a What do you think will happen if she makes the slope steeper?

b What do you think will happen if she makes the slope less steep?

c What are the input and outcome variables in this experiment?

d Is there a relationship between the variables? If you think there is, copy and complete this sentence to describe it.

The higher the slope, the _____ the car moves.

Pulling shoes

Kerry carried out an experiment. She attached a newtonmeter to a shoe and pulled it across the floor. She put different weights inside the shoe. Then she measured the extension of the spring on the newtonmeter when the pull was just enough to make the shoe move across the floor.

The table below shows the results of the experiment.

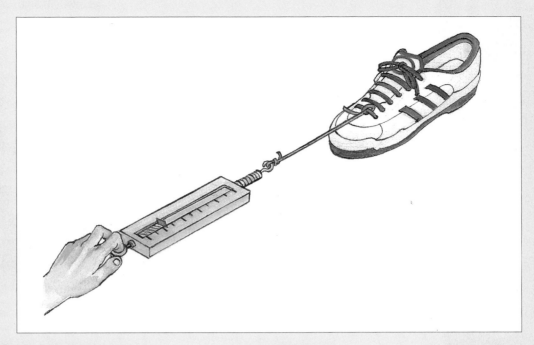

Weight in N	1	2	3	4	5
Extension of spring in mm	10	20	30	40	50

e What are the input and outcome variables in the experiment?

f Is there a relationship between the variables? if you think there is, copy and complete this sentence to describe it.

The more weight in the shoe, the _____ the extension of the spring in the newtonmeter.

Questions

1. Copy and complete these sentences.

We link variables together in _____.

When you throw a ball, the more _____ you use to throw the ball, the _____ it will go.

2. The table below shows the force used to push a go-kart and the distance it travelled.

Force in N	10	20	30	40	50
Distance in cm	5	10	15	20	25

a What are the input and outcome variables in the experiment?

b Is there a relationship between the variables? If you think there is, copy and complete this sentence to describe it.

The more force you use to push a go-kart, the _____ the go-kart will travel.

A day at the zoo

When will it be born?

Altaf and Rabeya were visiting the zoo one weekend. Mum had also brought along their baby sister Shammin.

Altaf loved watching the elephants. One of the elephants was expecting a baby. Altaf really liked baby elephants.

He wondered how long it would be before the baby elephant was born.

Dana his hamster was pregnant for three weeks. He asked his mum if they could come back next month and see the baby elephant. Mum said that it would not be born yet. Elephants are pregnant for nearly two years! Mum was only pregnant for nine months with Shammin. The length of time that an animal is pregnant is called its **gestation period**.

a Write the animals below in order of gestation period, starting with the longest.

human   hamster   elephant

First steps

They went to see the zebras. Rabeya was surprised to see a very small zebra trotting around with one of the other zebras. It was only born a few weeks ago. Shammin was six months old and still could not walk. Mum told her that lots of animals can walk very soon after they are born.

b Why do you think it is important for a baby zebra to be able to run soon after it is born?

Living in a pouch

They went to see the kangaroos. Altaf could see a baby kangaroo poking its head out of its mother's pouch. The zoo keeper told him that kangaroos are a special kind of mammal called a **marsupial**. These animals have a short pregnancy, and the baby is too helpless to survive on its own. It crawls into a special pouch and stays in there for another six months.

c How does the pouch allow the baby kangaroo to survive?

A baby kangaroo just after it is born.

Will it breed?

Everyone was very excited about the new panda. It had been flown in from a zoo in Germany. Giant pandas are getting very rare in the wild. The zoo hoped that the new panda would breed with one of their female pandas and produce a baby panda.

Questions

1. Copy and complete these sentences.

Very small animals, such as the hamster, have _____ pregnancies. Big animals, such as the elephant, have very _____ pregnancies. The amount of time that an animal is pregnant is called its g_____ p_____.

2. Draw a flow chart to show the life cycle of a human.

3. What do you think about zoos? Write a letter to *Wild Zone*, a nature magazine, either:

● explaining why zoos are good for animals

or

● explaining why you think zoos are bad, and what should be done to change them.

Spot the difference

Making sperm and eggs

The bodies of men and women have some very important differences. Men produce sex cells called **sperm**, and women produce sex cells called **eggs**. To make a baby, a sperm and an egg must join together.

The reproductive systems of a man and a woman are different because they have to do different jobs.

Male reproductive system

The picture opposite shows the male reproductive system. It is shown from the side.

Sperm are made in the **testes**. The photo below shows sperm seen under a microscope.

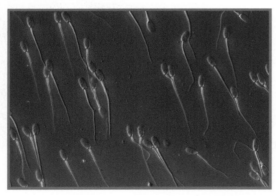

The testes are in a special bag of skin called the **scrotum**. This keeps the sperm at just the right temperature.

When the sperm leave the testes, they pass along a tube called the **sperm tube**. On the way the sperm pass two **glands**. These glands add a liquid to the sperm. The sperm and liquid together are called **semen**. Then the sperm pass down the **penis** where they leave the man's body.

Learn about

➤ Male and female reproductive systems

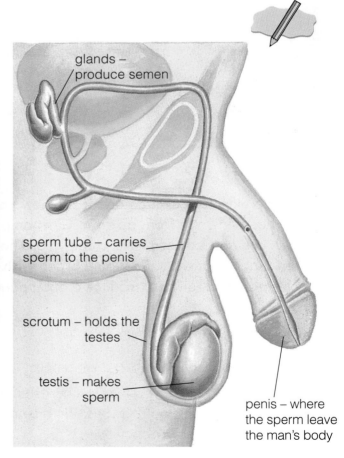

glands – produce semen

sperm tube – carries sperm to the penis

scrotum – holds the testes

testis – makes sperm

penis – where the sperm leave the man's body

a Where are sperm made?

b List the parts, in order, that the sperm go through on their way out of the man's body.

Female reproductive system

The female reproductive system is shown from the front.
The photo shows an egg.

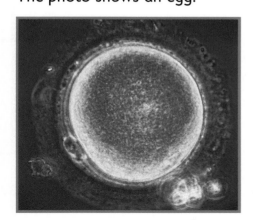

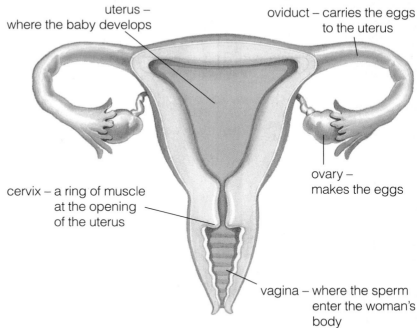

uterus –
where the baby develops

oviduct – carries the eggs
to the uterus

ovary –
makes the eggs

cervix – a ring of muscle
at the opening
of the uterus

vagina – where the sperm
enter the woman's
body

The eggs are made in the **ovaries**.
There are two ovaries, one on each
side. Once a month an egg leaves one
of the ovaries and passes down the
oviduct. The egg and sperm may meet
in the oviduct.

The **uterus** (womb) is where the baby will develop. The
opening of the uterus is called the **cervix**. This can open
quite wide to let the baby out when it is ready to be born.

c Where are the eggs made?

Questions

1. Copy and complete these sentences. Use words
   from the word wall to fill the gaps.

ovaries	testes	semen	uterus

oviduct	penis	sperm tube

   a Sperm are made in the _____. When
   the sperm leave the testes, they pass down the
   _____. Glands add a special liquid to
   make _____. The sperm then leave
   through the _____.

   b Eggs are made in the _____. Every
   month an egg is released and passes down the
   _____ to the _____.

2. What happens in the uterus?

3. **a** Some men may not want any more
   children. They can have an operation
   which closes up their sperm tubes.
   Why will this stop them having any
   more children?

   b A woman may have a similar
   operation. The oviducts are closed up.
   How will this stop her having babies?

   ### For your notes

   Sperm are made in the **testes**. They
   pass down the **sperm tube** and out
   of the **penis**.

   Eggs are made in the **ovaries**. They
   pass down the **oviduct** to the **uterus**.

125

A new generation

How the sperm and egg meet

To make a baby, the male and female sex cells must meet and join together. When a man and a woman make love, the man's penis enters the woman's vagina. Sperm are released from the penis into the vagina. This is how the sperm get into the body of the woman. It is called **sexual intercourse**. The sperm then swim towards the egg.

a What two cells must meet to make a baby?

b How do the sperm get into the woman's body?

Learn about

➤ Fertilisation

Did you know?
Up to 500 million sperm are released into the vagina.

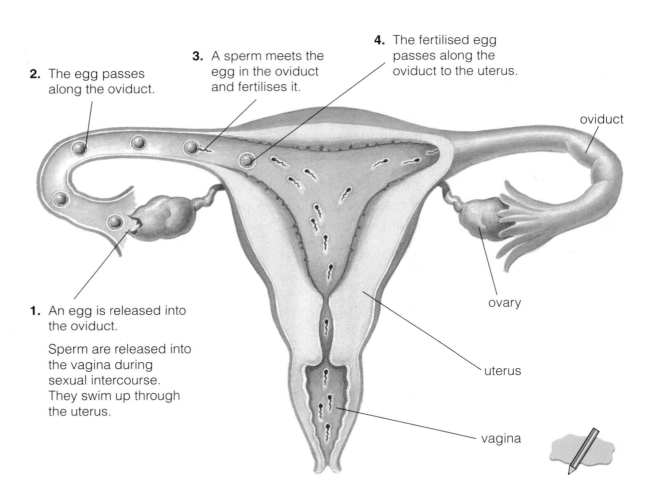

2. The egg passes along the oviduct.

3. A sperm meets the egg in the oviduct and fertilises it.

4. The fertilised egg passes along the oviduct to the uterus.

oviduct

ovary

uterus

vagina

1. An egg is released into the oviduct.

Sperm are released into the vagina during sexual intercourse. They swim up through the uterus.

What happens to the sperm?

What happens next depends on whether an egg has been released into the oviduct.

● The sperm start to swim from the vagina into the uterus. Many sperm die on the way.

● The sperm swim up through the uterus and then into both oviducts.

If there is no egg in the oviducts:

- All the sperm will die in a short time.
- No baby will be produced.

If there is an egg in the oviducts:

- The sperm will surround it, as shown in photo **A**.
- The first sperm to reach the egg burrows into it. Photo **B** shows this.
- The nucleus of the sperm joins with the nucleus of the egg. This is called **fertilisation**.
- The fertilised egg will become a baby. The woman is pregnant.

c Explain what fertilisation means.

d What happens to the sperm if there is no egg in the oviducts?

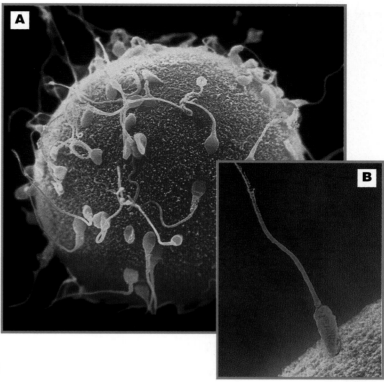

Twins

Sometimes a woman gives birth to more than one baby at the same time. Two babies together are called **twins**. Twins can be produced in two ways.

Identical twins, like Hannah and Mary, come from just one egg. The egg splits into two just after it starts to develop into a baby. Because both Hannah and Mary came from the same egg and sperm, they look exactly the same.

Non-identical twins, like Charlie and Amy, are produced if two eggs are released at the same time. Each egg is then fertilised by a different sperm. These twins are no more alike or different than any other brothers and sisters.

Questions

1. Why do you think so many sperm are produced?

2. Imagine that you are a sperm. Write a story about your journey to the egg.

3. Give one difference in the way identical twins and non-identical twins are produced.

For your notes

In **sexual intercourse**, millions of sperm are released into the woman's vagina. Most will die, but one may make it to the egg.

Fertilisation happens when the nucleus of a sperm joins up with the nucleus of an egg.

Pregnancy

From egg to baby

After an egg is fertilised, it settles in the thick, soft lining of the uterus. This is called **implantation**. It grows into a tiny ball of cells called the **embryo**. When this happens the woman is **pregnant**. The embryo then grows more to become a **fetus**.

a What is an embryo?

b When is the woman pregnant?

Learn about

➤ Pregnancy

➤ Birth

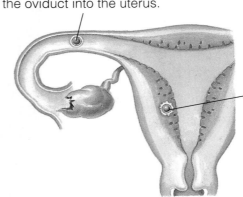

The fertilised egg passes along the oviduct into the uterus.

Implantation – it settles in the spongy lining of the uterus.

The growing baby

The photos show the development of the fetus during **pregnancy**.

At about 4 weeks the baby's heart starts to beat.

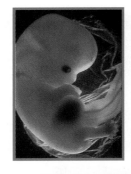

By about 9 weeks, the baby has a head, arms and legs. Fingers and toes start to develop.

At around 22 weeks, the doctor can hear the baby's heartbeat. Its lungs are starting to develop. Its mother will feel it kicking.

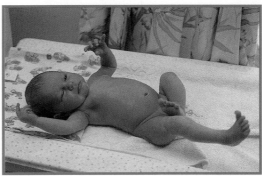

At 39 weeks, when it is born, the baby is fully developed. It has a lot of fat to keep it warm when it is born.

c What differences can you see between the pictures at 4 weeks and 39 weeks?

Getting what it needs

The embryo gets all the substances it needs from the mother's body. It does this through the **placenta**. This forms in the uterus early in pregnancy. The embryo is linked to the placenta by the **cord**. Blood in the cord carries substances to and fro.

The embryo gets food and oxygen from the placenta, through the cord. It gets rid of carbon dioxide and other waste substances to the placenta, through the cord.

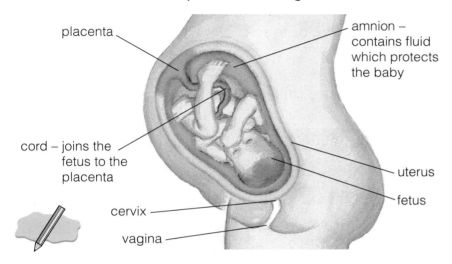

placenta

amnion – contains fluid which protects the baby

cord – joins the fetus to the placenta

uterus

fetus

cervix

vagina

d What links the baby to the placenta?

e What is the job of the placenta?

Birth

Pregnancy lasts for about nine months. Then the baby is fully developed and ready to be born. It is pushed out of the uterus by **contractions**. These happen when the strong muscles of the uterus wall squeeze.

After it is born, the baby is still attached to the mother by the cord. The cord has to be cut and tied. The placenta is no longer needed and leaves the uterus a few minutes later. This is called the **afterbirth**. The mother produces milk as food for the baby. The baby gets its oxygen from breathing air.

f How long is pregnancy?

g What is the afterbirth?

h Why is the afterbirth no longer needed?

Questions

1. Write out each part along with its correct job.

Parts	Jobs
amnion	joins the placenta to the fetus
cord	supplies the fetus with food and oxygen
placenta	pushed out of the uterus after the baby is born
afterbirth	protects the baby from bumps

2. Copy and complete these sentences.

   Pregnancy lasts about _____ months. The baby is pushed out by the strong _____ of the uterus. The _____ that joins the baby to the placenta is cut and tied when the baby is born. The _____ also comes out of the uterus a few minutes later. This is known as the _____.

3. Make a leaflet for Year 6 pupils describing how the baby develops inside the mother and is born after nine months. Look at the pictures and text on these pages to help you.

For your notes

It takes nine months for a human baby to develop fully inside its mother. This is called **pregnancy**.

Adolescence

All change!

Adolescence is a time in everyone's life when physical and emotional changes happen. The changes prepare us to be young adults. The changes happen at different times in different people.

Puberty is the first part of adolescence. Most of the physical changes take place during puberty. Puberty usually starts earlier in girls than in boys. Young people often find that their emotions and behaviour change. They become more attracted to the opposite sex.

a What happens in adolescence?

b What is the first part of adolescence called?

During puberty

Many changes happen to boys and girls in puberty. **Hormones** are substances that make these changes happen.

c What are hormones?

The changes that happen at puberty are given in the table. Some are also shown in the picture below.

Changes in boys	Changes in girls
Sudden increase in height (growth spurt)	Sudden increase in height (growth spurt)
Hair starts to grow on body, including pubic hair	Hair starts to grow on body, including pubic hair
Voice deepens	Breasts grow
Testes start to make sperm and hormones	Ovaries start to release eggs and make hormones
Shoulders broaden	Hips widen
Sexual organs get bigger	Periods start

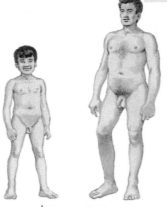

boy → man

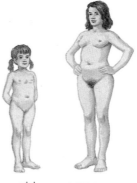
girl → woman

d What is the job of the testes?

e What happens in the ovaries at puberty?

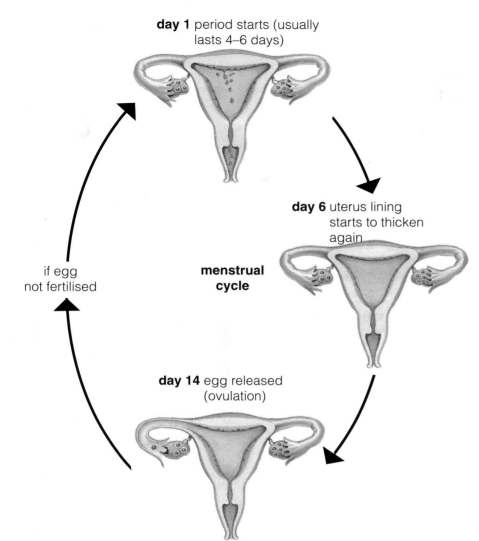

day 1 period starts (usually lasts 4–6 days)

day 6 uterus lining starts to thicken again

menstrual cycle

if egg not fertilised

day 14 egg released (ovulation)

The menstrual cycle

During puberty, girls start a monthly cycle called the **menstrual cycle**. The cycle lasts about 28 days. Hormones cause an egg to develop and be released. The lining of the uterus builds up.

If the egg is fertilised, it is implanted in this lining. If the egg is not fertilised, the lining is not needed for the embryo. The lining made of dead cells and blood breaks down and leaves the body through the vagina. This is known as a **period**. The diagram opposite shows the menstrual cycle.

f How long is the menstrual cycle?

g What is a period?

When the girl's period finishes, a new egg will develop in the ovary and the cycle continues. A woman stops having periods while she is pregnant.

Questions

1. Write out each word along with its explanation.

Words

period   puberty   adolescence

Explanations

- a time in everyone's life when physical and emotional changes take place
- the first part of adolescence in which most of these changes take place
- dead cells and blood leave the body through the vagina

2. a Describe three changes that happen to boys during puberty.

b Describe three changes that happen to girls during puberty.

3. What happens next in the menstrual cycle if an egg is not fertilised?

For your notes

Adolescence is a time when physical and emotional changes happen.

Puberty is the first part of adolescence when most of the physical changes happen.

Pregnant pause

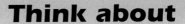

Time to develop

An elephant is pregnant for a lot longer than a hamster. You are going to find out why this happens. The table shows some data about the length of time that different animals are pregnant. The animals are in order of size, with the smallest animal first.

a Plot a bar chart of this data. Think carefully about the scale you use.

b Which is the biggest animal?

c Which is the smallest animal?

d Which animal has the longest pregnancy?

e Which animal has the shortest pregnancy?

Look carefully at your graph. Can you see a pattern in your results?

f Altaf thinks that there is no relationship between the size of animal and its gestation period. Do you agree with him? Explain your answer.

Animal	Gestation period in days
Mouse	21
Squirrel	30
Cat	62
Kangaroo	40
Ape	200
Human	280
Camel	355
Rhino	420
Elephant	649

g Look at your graph again. Is there any animal that doesn't fit the pattern?

h What do you know about this animal that might explain this?

Predators and prey

One way of putting animals in order of size is to measure their mass. Here is some data for three more animals. They are all predators.

Animal	Average adult mass in kg	Gestation period in days
Cheetah	95	60
Lion	190	108
Tiger	210	109

i Draw a line graph of this data. Put adult mass along the bottom and gestation period up the side. Use blue to plot the points and join them up with a curved line. Label the line 'predators'.

This table shows data for three prey animals.

Animal	Average adult mass in kg	Gestation period in days
Antelope	45	180
Wildebeest	200	255
Zebra	280	360

j Add this data to your graph. Use red to plot these points and join them with a curved line. Label this line 'prey'.

k Which line is higher on your graph, the predators one or the prey one?

l What does this tell you?

When a lion cub is born, it is blind and helpless for a week or so. It cannot move very far, and its mother has to look after it. A baby zebra is very different. It can walk with the rest of the herd only a few hours after it is born.

The longer a baby animal spends inside its mother, the more developed it will be.

m A zebra spends a lot longer developing inside its mother than a lion does. How does this help the zebra?

133

adaptation Having features that help a living thing to survive in a particular place.

adapted A well adapted organism has features that help it to survive in a particular place.

adolescence The time in a young person's life when physical and emotional changes happen.

afterbirth The placenta comes out of the uterus after the baby is born. It is called the afterbirth.

air resistance The friction a moving object makes with air.

ammeter An instrument to measure current.

amphibians One of the groups of vertebrate animals. Amphibians lay eggs in water but breathe air. They have a smooth moist skin.

amplitude The distance between the top of a vibration and the middle of the vibration.

amps Current is measured in amps. The short way of writing amps is A.

animal cells The building blocks that make up all animals. Animal cells have a cell membrane, cytoplasm and a nucleus.

anther The part of the stamen in a flower that makes the pollen.

arthropods Group of invertebrate animals with segmented bodies and jointed legs.

atom The smallest part of an element.

attract To pull together.

bacteria A group of microorganisms. Some bacteria cause disease.

balanced forces Two forces of the same size pulling in opposite directions.

birds One of the groups of vertebrate animals. Birds lay eggs with a hard shell, look after their young and have feathers and wings.

blubber A thick layer of fat that some animals have to help them keep warm.

camouflage Features that help a living thing to blend in with its surroundings.

carbon dioxide A compound made when carbon burns and joins with oxygen.

carbon An element that is in coal and other fuels.

carpel The female parts of a flower, that produce the egg cells.

cathode ray oscilloscope A machine that shows vibrations as a squiggle on a screen. Cathode ray oscilloscope may be written as CRO for short.

cell membrane A thin layer that surrounds the cell and controls the movement of substances in and out.

cell wall A tough box around plant cells.

cells Tiny building blocks that make up all living things.

cellulose A tough stringy substance found in plant cell walls.

centipedes One of the groups of arthropods. Centipedes have lots of legs and a segmented body.

cervix A ring of muscle at the opening of the uterus.

change of state Changing from a solid to a liquid or a liquid to a gas and back again.

chemical change A change that makes a new substance. Many chemical changes are irreversible.

chemical energy Energy stored in a material, which will be given out in a chemical reaction.

chemical reaction A change that makes a new substance.

chloride A compound that contains chlorine atoms.

chlorophyll A green substance that is needed for photosynthesis.

chloroplasts The parts of a plant cell that carry out photosynthesis.

chromatography A method used to separate mixtures of substances. The most soluble substances travel the furthest up the paper.

circuit Batteries and lamps joined up by wires to make a closed loop.

classification Putting things with similar features into the same group.

combustion The chemical reaction that happens when something burns.

complete circuit Batteries and lamps joined up by wires to make a closed loop.

compound microscope A microscope that uses more than one lens to magnify things.

compound A substance that contains more than one type of atom joined together.

condensing Changing from a gas to a liquid.

conduct To pass along. Heat energy can be conducted. Electrical energy can be conducted.

conductor A material that passes along heat energy is a good conductor of heat energy. A material that passes along electrical energy is a good conductor of electricity.

conservation of energy The idea that energy is passed from place to place but is hard to create or destroy.

contractions The muscles of the uterus wall squeeze when a baby is born.

copper oxide The compound that is made when copper burns and joins with oxygen in the air.

cord This links the developing baby to the placenta in a pregnant female mammal.

core A magnetic material put inside a coil to make an electromagnet.

corrosion The process by which metals change over time. Rusting is one sort of corrosion.

crustaceans One of the groups of arthropods. Crustaceans have lots of legs, a soft body and usually a hard shell.

current How fast the electricity goes around the circuit.

cytoplasm A jelly-like substance found inside cells.

decibel Loudness of sound is measured in decibels. The short way of writing decibels is dB.

dense A dense material has a lot of particles in a small volume.

density How heavy a material is for its size.

dissolve The particles of a solid break apart and mix with the particles of a liquid.

distillation A method used to separate mixtures of liquids with different boiling points.

distilled water Water that has been made pure. It has been changed to a gas and condensed back to a liquid again.

eardrum A small 'drumskin' inside the ear which vibrates when sounds reach it.

egg cell The female sex cell in a plant. An egg cell joins with a pollen grain to make an embryo plant.

egg The female sex cell in an animal. An egg joins with a sperm to make a baby.

electrical energy Energy carried by electricity.

electromagnet A coil of wire with an iron core and a current through the wire.

electron microscope A microscope that uses electrons instead of light. It makes things look very much larger.

element A substance that contains only one type of atom.

embryo A tiny ball of cells formed from the fertilised egg in animal reproduction.

embryo plant A new plant inside a seed ready to grow.

energy conservation The idea that energy is passed from place to place but is hard to create or destroy.

energy transfer The movement of energy from one place to another.

energy When anything happens, energy is transferred. Energy makes things work.

evaporating Changing from a liquid to a gas.

extension The amount a spring stretches when you hang a weight on it.

features Special parts of organisms, or particular things they do.

fertilisation In an animal, a sperm joining with an egg to make a baby. In a plant, a pollen grain joining with an egg cell to make an embryo plant.

fetus A developing baby inside the uterus of a female mammal.

filament Part of the stamen in a flower. The filament supports the anther.

filament lamp An electric light with a piece of wire that forms part of the circuit. The wire glows when electricity passes through it.

fish One of the groups of vertebrate animals. Fish live in water and lay eggs there. They breathe through gills and have scales and fins.

flammable A flammable material burns easily.

flatworms One of the groups of invertebrate animals. Flatworms have a flat leaf-shaped body.

force arrows Arrows we draw that point in the direction of a force. The length shows the size of the force.

freezing Changing from a liquid to a solid.

frequency The number of vibrations that happen in a second.

friction The force that is made when things rub together.

fruit A structure made in a flower, that contains the seed. It is formed from the ovary.

fuel A material that has a lot of stored chemical energy. We burn a fuel to use the energy.

fuel consumption The amount of fuel a vehicle uses to travel a certain distance. Fuel consumption is measured in kilometres per litre or miles per gallon.

gas A state of matter that is not very dense. A gas is easily squashed. Its shape and volume can change.

gestation period The time a baby takes to develop inside its mother before it is born.

glands Parts that make hormones and other substances in animals. In male animals, the glands in the reproductive system make a liquid which mixes with sperm to make semen.

gravitational energy Energy stored because something is lifted up.

gravity The force that pulls everything towards the centre of the Earth. The other planets, the Moon and the Sun also pull things because of gravity.

greenhouse effect The carbon dioxide in the air stops some of the heat energy escaping from the Earth. It behaves like the glass in a greenhouse. The greenhouse effect may increase, making the Earth warmer.

group A verical column in the periodic table.

habitat The place where an animal lives.

heat energy Energy transferred from a hot object to a cooler object.

hertz Frequency is measured in hertz. The short way of writing hertz is Hz.

hormone A substance in the body that makes changes happen.

hydrocarbon A substance that contains only carbon and hydrogen atoms.

identical twins Two babies that came from the same sperm and egg. They are born at the same time and they look exactly the same.

implantation In animal reproduction, a fertilised egg settles into the soft lining of the uterus.

inherited features Features that are passed on from the parents.

input variable The thing you change in an investigation.

insects One of the groups of arthropods. Insects have six legs and three parts to the body.

insoluble A substance that is insoluble will not dissolve.

invertebrate An animal without a backbone.

iron oxide The compound that is made when iron burns and joins with oxygen in the air.

irreversible change A change that cannot be changed back to how it was before.

jellyfish One of the groups of invertebrate animals. Jellyfish have a soft jelly-like body.

joules Energy is measured in joules. The short way of writing joules is J.

kilogram Mass is measured in kilograms. The short way of writing kilograms is kg.

kilohertz There are 1000 hertz in 1 kilohertz. The short way of writing kilohertz is kHz.

kilojoules There are 1000 joules in 1 kilojoule. The short way of writing kilojoules is kJ.

light energy Energy transferred by light.

light microscope Another name for a compound microscope.

limewater A solution used to test for carbon dioxide. Limewater turns milky when carbon dioxide bubbles through it.

liquid A state of matter that flows. The shape of a liquid can change, but its volume is fixed.

loudness The volume of a sound. The more energy the sound has, the louder it is.

lubricant A substance that reduces friction by making surfaces run smoothly against each other.

magnesium oxide The compound that is made when magnesium burns and joins with oxygen in the air.

magnet An object that makes a magnetic field.

magnetic field A space where magnetic materials are pulled.

magnetic field line The lines that iron filings make when they are in a magnetic field.

magnetic material A material that is attracted by a magnet.

magnification Making something look bigger.

mammals One of the groups of vertebrate animals. Mammals have hairy skin. Their babies develop inside the mother and are fed on milk.

mammary glands Features that female mammals have, that make milk.

marsupial A type of mammal. The baby develops in its mother's pouch.

mass A measure of how much matter an object has.

material Anything that is made up of particles. A material may be an element, a compound or a mixture.

matter Anything that has mass is made up of matter. Matter contains particles.

melting Changing from a solid to a liquid.

menopause Time in a woman's life when her periods stop.

menstrual cycle A monthly cycle in women. During the cycle an egg is released, and the woman has a period.

metal A material that is shiny and conducts electrical and heat energy.

microorganism A very small living thing that can only be seen with a microscope.

microscope A device that is used for looking at very small objects.

millipedes One of the groups of arthropods. Millipedes have lots of legs and a segmented body.

mixture A material that contains more than one substance.

model An idea or picture made up by a scientist to show a situation that cannot be seen. A model helps scientists think through explanations.

molluscs One of the groups of invertebrate animals. Molluscs have a soft muscular body with a foot, and usually a hard shell.

moulting Hair or feathers fall off an animal when it moults.

movement energy When something moves, it has movement energy.

newton Force is measured in newtons. The short way of writing newtons is N.

non-identical twins Two babies that came from different sperm and eggs. They are born at the same time, but look different.

non-metal A material that is not a metal.

nucleus The part of a cell that controls everything the cell does.

organism A living thing, that carries out the processes of life.

outcome variable The thing that changes during an investigation. The outcome variable is the thing you measure.

ovary In an animal, part of the female reproductive system that makes the eggs. In a plant, part of the carpel that makes the egg cells.

oviduct A tube in the reproductive system of a female animal. The eggs travel down the oviduct to the uterus.

oxide A compound that contains oxygen atoms. An oxide is made when a substance burns and joins with oxygen in the air.

oxygen One of the gases in the air. We need oxygen to stay alive, and burning uses oxygen.

palisade cells The cells in a leaf where photosynthesis takes place.

parallel circuit A circuit with more than one loop.

particles Tiny parts that make up every type of matter.

penis Part of the reproductive system in a male animal. The penis allows the sperm to be placed inside the vagina.

period A horizontal row in the periodic table

period Part of a woman's menstrual cycle. The lining of the uterus breaks down and leaves the body through the vagina.

periodic table The table showing all the elements.

photosynthesis Plants make food by photosynthesis. They turn carbon dioxide and water into sugars and oxygen, using light energy.

physical change A change in which no new substance is made. A change of state is a physical change. Physical changes are reversible.

pitch How high (squeaky) or low (bass) a sound is.

placenta Structure formed in a pregnant female mammal. The developing baby gets its food and oxygen from the placenta.

plant cells The building blocks that make up all plants. Plant cells have a cell membrane, cytoplasm and a nucleus, and also a cell wall, chloroplasts and a vacuole.

pollen grain The male sex cell in a plant. A pollen grain joins with an egg cell to make an embryo plant.

pollination The transfer of pollen from an anther to a stigma in plant reproduction.

pregnant A female animal is pregnant when there is a baby growing inside her uterus.

property How something looks, or how it behaves. The properties of a material include its colour, strength and hardness.

puberty The first part of adolescence, when physical changes happen.

pure A pure material only contains one substance.

range The different values that are possible, such as all the different heights in a group of people.

reaction A change in which a new substance is made.

reaction force A force that stops things falling through a solid object. When you sit on a chair, your weight is balanced by the reaction force from the chair.

relationship A pattern that links variables together. A relationship describes how the outcome variable changes when the input variable is changed.

repel To push apart.

reptiles One of the groups of vertebrate animals. Reptiles breathe air and lay eggs on land. They have a scaly dry skin.

reversible change A change that can be changed back to how it was before.

root hairs Tiny structures on a root that absorb water from the soil.

roundworms One of the groups of invertebrate animals. Roundworms have a soft thin round body.

rust The substance that is formed when iron is exposed to air and water. Rust is iron oxide.

saturated A solution is saturated when no more of a substance can dissolve in it.

scale diagram A drawing that shows something bigger or smaller than it really is.

scale factor A number used in scale drawing. You multiply by the scale factor to scale something up. You divide by the scale factor to scale it down.

scaling down Making something smaller.

scaling up Making something bigger.

scrotum Part of the reproductive system in a male animal. The scrotum is a bag of skin that holds the testes.

seed A structure made in a flower, that contains the new embryo plant and a food store.

segmented worms One of the groups of invertebrate animals. Segmented worms have a soft ringed body.

segments Sections of the body in arthropods and segmented worms.

semen A mixture of sperm and a special liquid to help them swim.

series circuit A circuit in which everything is in one loop.

sexual intercourse The man's penis enters the woman's vagina, and sperm are released into the vagina.

solid A state of matter that is dense and has a fixed shape and volume.

soluble A substance that is soluble will dissolve.

solute The substance that dissolves to make a solution.

solution A mixture of a solute dissolved in a solvent.

solvent A liquid that substances can dissolve in.

sound energy Energy transferred by sound.

species A particular type of animal or plant. Members of a species can reproduce to form more of their kind.

speed How fast something is moving.

sperm tube A tube in the reproductive system of a male animal. Sperm swim from the testis to the penis through the sperm tube.

sperm The male sex cell in an animal. The sperm swims to the egg and joins with it to make a baby.

spiders One of the groups of arthropods. Spiders have eight legs and two parts to the body.

stainless steel A type of steel that does not rust.

stamens The male parts of a flower, that produce the pollen.

starfish One of the groups of invertebrate animals. Starfish have a hard star-shaped body.

states of matter The three states of matter are solids, liquids and gases.

stigma Part of the carpel in a flower. The pollen lands on the stigma.

stomata Holes in a leaf's surface. Gases get in and out of the leaf through the stomata.

strain energy Energy stored in a material because the material is being pulled or pushed.

streamlined A way of shaping things such as cars to keep air resistance low.

style Part of the carpel in a flower. The pollen tube grows down through the style.

substance A material that is always made up from the same atoms arranged in the same way. A substance may be an element or a compound.

sulphide A compound that contains sulphur atoms.

surroundings Everything around a living thing, including its diet and the way it lives.

symbol The letter or letters used to stand for an element.

testes Parts of the reproductive system in a male animal. The testes make the sperm. One on its own is called a testis.

transferring energy Moving energy from one place to another.

twins Two babies that develop together inside the mother and are born at the same time.

unbalanced forces Forces pushing in different directions when one force is bigger than the other. An unbalanced force makes the object move or speed up or slow down.

upthrust The force caused by water pushing up against an object.

uterus Part of the reproductive system in a female animal. The baby grows and develops in the uterus.

vacuole A bag inside plant cells that contains a liquid which keeps the cell firm.

vagina Opening to the reproductive system in a female animal. Sperm enter the woman's body through the vagina, and the baby leaves through the vagina when it is born.

value A measurement or observation.

variable A thing that we change or that changes in an investigation.

variation The differences between members of a species.

veins These transport water, minerals and sugars around a plant.

vertebrate An animal with a backbone.

vibrating Moving up and down or side to side.

vibration A movement up and down or side to side.

virus A group of microorganisms that cause disease.

voltage You get a voltage where energy enters or leaves a circuit.

voltmeter An instrument used to measure voltage.

volts Voltage is measured in volts. The short way of writing volts is V.

water vapour Water that has turned to a gas.

weight The force of gravity on an object, that makes it feel heavy.

word equation An equation in words to show a chemical reaction.

Note: page numbers in **bold** show where a word is **explained** in the text. Words are also explained in the Glossary on pages 134–43.

A

adaptation **44–5**, 46–7, 134
adapted 134
adolescence **130**, 131, 134
afterbirth **129**, 134
air
   and burning **50**
   resistance **113**, 115, 134
   sound travels through 13
aluminium 76, 77, 94, 95, 101
ammeter **66**, 134
amphibians **39**, 134
amplitude **14**, 134
amps (A) **66**, 134
animals 36, 42–3
   Arctic **44–5**
   cells 79, **80**, 81, 134
   reproduction 38–9, **122–3**, **132–3**
   speed 118–19
anther **88**, 134
Arctic 37, **44–7**
arthropods **41**, 134
ash and soot 49, 52
atom **96**, 134
attract **75**, 134

B

babies *see* reproduction
backbones, animals without and with
   see invertebrates; vertebrates
bacteria **36**, 134
balanced forces **116**, 117, 134
balloon 20–1, 23, 117
batteries 64, 65, 66–7, 69, 70, 76
biodome experiment 61
birds 37, **38**, 112, 134
birth **129**
birthday party 20–1

blubber **45**, 134
bonfire 8, 48–9
bow and arrow 8
brakes 112
brass 94, 96
breathing *see* respiration
bromine 99, 101
bronze 92, 93, 96
burning **48–61**
   changes after 52–3
   particles and reactions 58–9
   relationships between variables 60–1
   things needed for 50–1
   see also fuel

C

camouflage **44**, 134
candles 21, 48, 50, 55
carbon 134
   in compounds 107
   filaments, electric 62–3
   forms **101**
   as fuel (coal and charcoal) 55, 56, **57**, 58–60
   properties 100, 101
carbon dioxide 134
   atoms in **107**
   and burning **57**, 58–9, 60
   and plants 82, 83, 84, 85
   and temperature 60–1
carpel **88**, 134
cars 112, 120
   and energy 17
   fuel for (petrol) 55, 59
   rusting 104
   speed 113, 115
cathode ray oscilloscope (CRO) **14**, 135
cats 119, 132, 133

cells **78**, **80**, 135
  animal 79, **80**, 81, 134
  cell membrane **80**, 134
  cell wall 80, **81**
  plant **80**, 81, **84**, **85**, 140
cellulose **81**, 135
centipedes **41**, 135
cervix **125**, 129, 135
change of state **20–33**, 135
  analysing results 32–3
  condensing 27, 135
  dissolving 28–9, 136
  evaporating 27, 136
  freezing 26, 137
  melting 26, 139
  particles 24–7, 140
  separating mixtures 30–1
  see also gas; liquid; solid
charcoal 55, 56
cheetahs 119, 133
chemical changes 141
  see also chemical reactions
chemical energy **8–9**, 17, 135
  in food 10–11
  in fuel **55**
  transferring 16
chemical reactions (chemical changes)
  135
  and burning **52–3**, **58–9**
  metals 102–3
chloride **103**, 135
chlorine 98, 99, 101, 103
chlorophyll **80**, **83**, 84, 85, 135
chloroplasts **80**, 82–3, 84, 85, 135
chromatography **31**, 32–3, 135
chromium 94, 105
circuits **64–5**, 72–3, 135
  complete **64**, 135
  complicated 67–8
  parallel **72**, 73, 140
  series **72**, 73, 142
  symbols **65**, 66, 68

class and matches model 71
classification **36**, 37, 100–1, 135
cloud, energy in 16
coal 56–7, 58, 60
  truck model 70
cobalt 75, 97
colour
  and burning metals 53
  chromatography 31–3, 135
  in food 33
  of plants *see* chlorophyll
combustion **58**, 135
complete circuit **70**, 135
compound microscope **78**, 135
compounds **106–7**, 135
  see also oxides; water
condensing **27**, 135
conduct **94**, 135
conductor **94**, 135
conservation of energy **16**, 17, 135, 136
contractions **129**, 135
copper 92, 96, 97
  properties 76, 93, 94, 95, 101
copper oxide **53**, 135
cord **129**, 136
core **76**, 77, 136
crime and colours 32–3
crustaceans **41**, 136
current **66**, 67, 70, 72, 136
cytoplasm **80**, 136

D

decibel (dB) **14**, 136
dense and density **25**, 136
desert animals 45
dissolve and dissolving **28–9**, 136
distance and speed 118–19
distillation **30**, 136
distilled water **30**, 136

E

eardrum **12**, 136
egg cell in plant **88**, 89, 136

eggs, animal 38–9, **124**, 126–7, 128, 130, 136
electrical energy 3, **6**, 7, 12, 136
electricity **62–77**
  current **66**, 67, 136
  magnets and electromagnets 74–7
  metals conduct **94**
  models of 70–1
  series and parallel circuits 72–3, 140, 142
  voltage **68**, 69, 73, 143
  see also circuits; lamps
electromagnet **76–7**, 136
electron microscope **79**, 136
elements 136
  classifying 100–1
  non-metals 97, **98–101**, 140
  properties 93–5, 98–9
  see also metals
elephants 122, 132
embryo **128**, 136
embryo plant **89**, 136
energy **2–19**, 136
  conserving **16**, 17, 135, 136
  investigating 18–19
  from Sun 4, 16–17, 60
  transfer diagram 9, 64
  types of *see* chemical energy; electrical energy; gravitational energy; heat energy; light energy; movement energy; sound energy; stored energy; transferring energy
  see also burning; fuel
equation 59
  word **59**, 83, 103, 143
Eskimos 44–5
evaporating **27**, 136
extension **116**, 137

F

features **36**, 137, 138
fertilisation **89**, **126**, 127, 137
fetus **128**, 129, 137

filament (in flower) **88**, 137
filament lamp **62**, 63, 137
fire
  bonfire 8, 48–9
  coal 56
  firefighting 50
  triangle 51
  see also burning
fireworks 48, 52, 53
fish 37, **39**, 137
flammable materials **51**, 137
flatworms **40**, 137
floating 117
flowers 36, 88–9
food 34
  carbon in 57
  and change of state 20–1
  colourings 33
  energy from 2, 10–11, 16, 54, 57
  hydrogen in 59
  and living things 36
  party 20–1
forces **108–21**
  balanced **116**, 117, 134
  force arrows **114**, 115, 137
  friction 112–13, 114
  reaction **117**, 141
  relationships between variables 120–1
  speed 108, **118–19**, 120, 142
  unbalanced **115**, 143
  weight and mass 110–11, 114, 117, 121, 133, 139
freezing **26**, 27, **102**, 137
frequency **15**, 137
friction **112**, 113, 114, 137
fruit **89**, 137
fuel 2, **51**, **54**, 137
  consumption **113**, 137
  in industry 60
  investigating 18–19
  oil and petrol 55, 59, 60
  storing energy 54–5
  see also coal

G

gas **23**, 55, 57, 60, 137
  compounds **107**
  hydrogen 59, 101, 107
  lamps 63
  nitrogen 98, 102
  particles in 24
  properties 98
  water vapour **30**, 143
  see also oxygen
gestation period **122**, **128**, 132–3, 137
glands **124**, 137
gold 92, 93, 95, 96
gravitational energy **8**, 9, 17, 137
gravity 109, **110**, 111, 137
greenhouse effect **60**, 61, 137

H

habitat **44**, 138
hearing 14
  see also sound
heat energy 3, **5**, 8, 64, 138
  conducted 94
  and friction 112
  from fuel 54, 60
  transferring 6, 7, 16, 17
  see also burning
heating metals **102–3**
height 90–1, 130
helium 98, 99
hertz (Hz) **15**, 138
hormones **130**, 138
humans 36, 38, 42–3
  body size and height 46–7, 90–1, 130
  reproduction **124–9**, 132
  speed 119
hydrocarbons **59**, 138
  petrol and oil 55, 59, 60
hydrogen 59, 101, 107

I

identical twins **127**, 138
implantation **128**, 138
industry, fuels in 60
inherited features **43**, 138
inks 29
  separating 31–3
input variable **19**, 61, 121, 138
insects **41**, 89, 138
insoluble **29**, 138
Inuit people 44–5
invertebrates **37**, 40–1, 138
iron 96
  magnetic 75, 76, 77
  properties 93, 94, 95, 101
  pure 107
  rusting **104–5**
  symbol for 96–7
  wrought and cast 92, 93
  see also steel
iron oxide **53**, **104**, 105, 138
iron sulphide 103
irreversible change 52, **102**, 138
  see also chemical reactions

J

jellyfish **40**, 138
joules (J) **10**, 54, 138
jumping 9, 109

K

kangaroos 123, 132
kilogram (kg) **111**, 138
kilohertz (kHz) **15**, 138
kilojoules (kJ) **10**, 11, 54, 138

L

lamps
  circuits 64, 66, 68–70, 72
  filament **62**, 63, 137
  gas 63
  symbol for 65
leaves 84–5

legs 41
 animals without 40
lens of microscope 78–9
life story **122–33**
 adolescence 130–1
 graphs 132–3
 see also living things; reproduction
lifting 2, 17, **110**
light bulbs 62–3
 see also lamps
light energy 3, **4**, 8, 64, 138
 different from sound 13
 from fuel 54, 60
 and plants *see* photosynthesis
 speed of 119
 from Sun 16–17
 transferring 6, 7, 16
light microscope 138
limewater **57**, 138
lion 38, 133
liquid **22**, 23, 138
 compounds **107**
 metals as **95**
 particles in 24, 26
 properties 99
living things **34–47**
 adaptation 44–7, 134
 classification 36–7
 invertebrates **37**, 40–1, 138
 range of data 46–7
 variation and species 42–3, 142, 143
 vertebrates **37**, 38–9, 143
 see also animals; life story; plants;
  reproduction
loudness 3, 14, 138
lubricant **112**, 138

M

machines 112
magnesium 53, 102–3, 106
magnesium oxide **53**, **102–3**, **106**, 139
magnet **74**, 75–7, 139
magnetic field **74**, 139

magnetic field line **74**, 139
magnetic material **75**, **94**, 139
magnification **79**, 139
mammals **38**, 139
 see also life story
mammary glands **38**, 139
marsupial **123**, 139
mass 59, **111**, 133, 139
material 139
matter **22**, 139
 see also change of state; states of
  matter
measuring
 energy 10–11, 54, 138
 force 110, 115, 139
 frequency 15, 138
 mass 111, 138
 sound 14, 136
 speed 118–19
 temperature 18–19
melting **26**, 27, **102**, 139
 point 102
menopause 139
menstrual cycle **131**, 139
mercury 95, 101, 102
metals **92–7**, **100–7**, 139
 burning 52–3
 chemical changes 102–3
 classifying 101
 in compounds 106–7
 magnetic 75, 76, 77
 oxides **52–3**, 135, 138
 physical changes 102
 rusting 104–5
 see also elements
microorganisms **36**, 139
microscopes **78–9**, 138, 139
 compound **78**, 135
 electron **79**, 136
millipedes **41**, 139
mining, coal 56–7
mixture **31**, **107**, 139
 metal 94, 96
 separating 30–1

model 139
  of Earth 61
  of electricity **70**, 71
molluscs **40**, 139
Moon, gravity on 110, 111
moulting **45**, 139
movement 34
  and friction 112–14, 137
  lifting 2, 17, 110
  pushing and pulling 108, 114, 116, 121
  running and jumping 2, 9, 108, 109, 112
  speed 108, 118–19, 120, 142
  throwing 108, 120
movement energy 2, **4**, 8–9, 12, 17, 60, 139

N

newton (N) **110**, 139
nickel 75, 76
nitrogen 98, 104
non-identical twins **127**, 140
non-living things **36**
non-metals 97, **98–101**, 140
north pole of magnet **74**, 75
North Pole of world *see* Arctic
nucleus **80**, 140
number equation 59
nutrition *see* food

O

oil 59, 60
organism **36**, 140
  see also living things
oscilloscope **14**, 135
outcome variable **19**, 61, 121, 140
ovary **88**, 89, **125**, 126, 130, 140
oviduct **125**, 126, 128, 140
ovulation 131
oxides **52–3**, **103**, 135, 138, 140
  hydrogen *see* water
  see also **carbon dioxide**

oxygen 140
  and burning **50**, 58–9
  in compounds 59, 107
  from plants 82, 83, 85
  properties 98
  and rusting 104–5
  uses 50, 99

P

palisade cells 84, **85**, 140
parachutes 113
parallel circuit **72**, 73, 140
particles **24–5**, 140
  and burning 58–9
  moving **26–7**
penis 12, **124**, 140
period 130, **131**, 140
periodic table **97**, 140
petrol 55, 59
photosynthesis 80, **82**, 83–5, 140
physical change **102**, 140
pitch **15**, 140
placenta **129**, 140
plants **36**, **80–9**
  cells **80**, 81, 84, **85**, 140
  flowers 36, 88–9
  reproduction 88–9
  and water 82, 84, 86–7
platinum and electricity 62
polar bear 44
pollen grain **88**, 89, 140
pollination **89**, 140
predators and prey 133
pregnancy and pregnant 122, **128**, 129, 132–3, 141
properties **22**, 23, 141
  of elements **92**, 93–5, 98–9, 101
puberty **130**, 131, 141
pulling 108, 116, 121
pure **30**, **107**, 141
pushing 108, 114

R

range 46–7, 141
reaction 141
  see also chemical reactions
reaction force **117**, 141
relationships between variables **18**, 141
  and burning **60–1**
  forces **120**, 121
  see also variables
repel **75**, 141
reproduction 34
  animals 38–9, **122–3**, **132–3**
  birth **129**
  fertilisation **126–7**
  human **124–9**, 132
  plants **88–9**
  pregnancy and gestation period 122,
    128, 129, 132–3
  reproductive systems **124–5**
reptiles **39**, 141
respiration (breathing) 34, 39, 50
reversible change **102**, 141
robots 34–5
root hairs **86**, 141
roots 86–7
roundworms **40**, 141
running 2, 108, 112
rust **104–5**, 141

S

saturated **28**, 141
scale diagram **90**, 141
scale factor **91**, 141
scaling down and up **90**, 91, 141
scrotum **124**, 141
seal 37, 44, 45
seed **89**, 141
segmented worms **40**, 141
segments **41**, 142
semen **124**, 142
separating mixtures **30–1**
series circuit **72**, 73, 142

sexual intercourse **126**, 142
silver 92, 95, 96, 97
sinking 117
skin 39, 79
sodium chloride 103, **106**
solid **22**, 23, 142
  compounds **106**
  metals as **95**
  particles in 24, 26
  properties 99
soluble **29**, 142
solute **28**, 142
solution **28**, 142
solvent **28**, 29, 142
sound energy 3, **4**, 12–15, 142
  transferring 6, 7, 12–13
south pole of magnet **74**, 75
species **42**, 142
speed 108, **118–19**, 120, 142
sperm **124**, 126–7, 130, 142
sperm tube **124**, 142
spiders 36, **41**, 142
stainless steel **105**, 142
stamens **88**, 142
starfish 37, **40**, 142
states of matter 142
  see also change of state; gas; liquid;
    solid
steel 92, 96, 105, 107
  properties 76, 93
  stainless **105**, 142
stigma **88**, 89, 142
stomata **85**, 142
stored energy **8–11**
  see also fuel
strain energy **8**, 9, 142
streamlined **113**, 142
style **88**, 89, 142
substance 142
  see also compounds; elements
sugar 28–9, 83, 87, 107
sulphide **103**, 142
sulphur 99, 101, 103
Sun, energy from 4, 16–17, 60

surroundings **43**, 143
symbols
  circuit **65**, 66, 68
  for elements **96–7**, 143

T

temperature
  and carbon dioxide 60–1
  measuring 18–19
  see also heat
testes **124**, 130, 143
three states of matter *see* gas; liquid;
  solid
throwing 108, 120
time and speed 118–19
tin 95, 105
transferring energy **6–7**, 12–13, 16, 64,
  136, 143
tungsten 63, 97
twins **127**, 138, 143

U

unbalanced forces **115**, 143
upthrust **117**, 143
uterus (womb) **125**, 126, 128–9, 131,
  143

V

vacuole 80, **81**, 143
vacuum 13
vagina 125, 126, 129, 143
value 143
  see also measuring
variables **120**, 143
  input **18**, 61, 121, 138
  outcome **18**, 61, 121, 140
  see also relationships
variation **42–3**, 143
veins of plants 84, **87**, 143
vertebrates **37**, 38–9, 143
vibrating **26**, 143
vibration **12**, 13, 15, 143
virus **36**, 143

voltage **68**, 69, 70, 73, 143
voltmeter **68**, 69, 143
volts (V) **68**, 143

W

water 59
  atoms in **107**
  dissolving in **28–9**, 136
  distilled **30**, 136
  hydrogen and oxygen in 59
  and plants 82, 84, 86–7
  pure **30**, 141
  and rusting 104–5
  sound travels through 13
water vapour **30**, 143
weight **110**, 111, 114, **117**, 121, 143
wood 13, 57
word equation **59**, 83, 103, 143
worms **40**, 137, 141

Z

zebra 122, 133
zinc 94, 95, 96
zoos 122–3

The authors and publishers would like to thank the following for permission to use photographs:

Cover photos: Tower arch, Tony Stone Images. **Blue spotted coral trout**, Oxford Scientific Films/Mark Webster. **Radio telescope at night**, Science Photo Library/David Nunuk.

1.1a, Gareth Boden. **1.1b**, Empics. **1.1c**, Empics. **1.1d**, J. Allan Cash Ltd. **1.1e**, Robert Harding Picture Library. **1.1f**, J. Allan Cash Ltd. **1.1g**, Trevor Hill. **1.1h**, Tony Stone Images. **1.2**, Robert Harding. **1.4 x 3**, Alan Edwards. **1.6a**, J. Allan Cash Ltd. **1.6b**, Kobal Collection. **1.7**, Holt Studios. **2.2a**, Trevor Hill. **2.2b**, Gareth Boden. **2.2c**, Tony Stone Images. **2.2d**, Science Photo Library/Richard Folwell. **2.5a-b**, Gareth Boden. **2.6**, Tony Stone Images. **3.2a**, Still Pictures/Ron Gilling. **3.2b**, Still Pictures/Francois Gilson. **3.2c**, Oxford Scientific Films/Harry Taylor. **3.2d**, Hans Reinhard. **3.2e**, Oxford Scientific Films/John Downer. **3.2f**, Oxford Scientific Films/Scott Camazine/CDC. **3.2g**, Science Photo Library/Dr. Linda Stannard. **3.2h**, Oxford Scientific Films/David M. Dennis. **3.2i**, Bruce Coleman. **3.3a-b**, PhotoDisc. **3.3c**, Oxford Scientific Films/Maurice Tibbles. **3.3d**, PhotoDisc. **3.3e**, Bruce Coleman. **3.3f**, FLPA/ Images of Nature/John Hawkins. **3.3g**, Oxford Scientific Films/Souricat. **3.3h**, Bruce Coleman. **3.3i**, Oxford Scientific Films/Max Gibbs. **3.4a**, Oxford Scientific Films/Fredrik Ehren Strom. **3.4b**, Bruce Coleman. **3.4c**, Oxford Scientific Films/Rudie Kuiter. **3.4d**, Oxford Scientific Films/London Scientific Film. **3.4e**, Oxford Scientific Films/David Fox. **3.4f**, FLPA/Images of Nature/Gerard Laci. **3.4g**, Oxford Scientific Films/Frank Schneidermever. **3.4h**, Bruce Coleman. **3.4i**, Bruce Coleman/Animal Ark. **3.4j**, Oxford Scientific Films/Mills Tandy. **3.5a**, NHPA/Darek Karp. **3.5b**, Oxford Scientific Films/Johnny Johnson. **3.5c**, Tony Stone Images. **3.6a**, Still Pictures/Fred Bruennar. **3.6b**, Oxford Scientific Films/Norbert Rosing. **3.6c**, Oxford Scientific Films/Colin Monteath. **3.6d**, Oxford Scientific Films/Mike Brown. **3.6e**, Oxford Scientific Films/Leszczynski. **4.1a-b**, J. Allan Cash Ltd. **4.1c**, Tony Stone Images. **4.2a**, Robert Harding Picture Library/Shout/P. Allen. **4.3a**, Peter Gould. **4.3a**, Robert Harding Picture Library. **4.3b**, Gareth Boden. **4.3c**, Peter Gould.**4.3d**, Gareth Boden. **4.4a**, Gareth Boden. **4.4b**, Tony Stone Images. **4.5a x 2**, Tony Stone Images. **4.5b**, Peter Gould. **4.7**, Robert Harding Picture Library. **5.1a**, Science Photo Library/Tek Image. **5.1b**, Mary Evans Picture Library. **5.1c**, Image Select/Ann Ronan. **5.1d**, Mary Evans Picture Library. **5.7a-b**, Gareth Boden. **5.7c-h**, Peter Gould. **5.8a**, Gareth Boden. **5.8b**, Robert Harding Picture Library/Shout/Hall. **6.1a**, Science Photo Library/Volker Steger, Peter Arnold Inc. **6.1b**, Gareth Boden. **6.1c**, Biophoto Associates. **6.2a**, Trevor Hill. **6.2b-c**, Biophoto Associates. **6.2d**, Science Photo Library/M.I. Walker. **6.3a**, Bruce Coleman. **6.4a**, Science Photo Library/Adam Hart Davis. **6.4b**, Biophoto Associates. **6.5a**, Holt Studios/Nigel Cattlin. **6.5b**, Biophoto Associates. **6.6a**, Holt Studios/Nigel Cattlin. **6.6b**, Science Photo Library/Andrew Syred. **7.1a-c, e**, Ancient Art & Architecture Collection. **7.1d**, J. Allan Cash Ltd. **7.1f**, Robert Harding Picture Library. **7.2a**, Gareth Boden. **7.2b**, Peter Gould. **7.2c-d**, Gareth Boden. **7.4a x 5**, Peter Gould. **7.4b**, Gareth Boden. **7.4c**, Robert Harding Picture Library. **7.6a**, Science Photo Library/Jerry Mason. **7.6b**, Peter Gould. **7.6c**, Gareth Boden. **7.7a**, Courtesy of Ford Motors. **7.7b**, Robert Harding Picture Library. **7.7c**, Collections/Brian Shuel. **7.7d**, Trevor Hill. **7.8a-d**, Gareth Boden. **8.3a**, Action Plus. **8.3b**, NHPA/Eric Soder. **8.3c-d**, The Stock Market. **8.3e**, Courtesy of Ford Motors. **9.1a**, Oxford Scientific Films/Edwin Sadd. **9.1b**, Zoological Society of London. **9.1c**, Bruce Coleman. **9.1d**, NHPA/A.N.T. **9.1e**, Bruce Coleman. **9.2a**, Sally & Richard Greenhill. **9.2b**, Science Photo Library/Science Pictures. **9.2c**, Science Photo Library/Andy Walker, Midland Fertility Service. **9.3a**, Science Photo Library/D. Phillips. **9.3b**, Science Photo Library/Don Fawcett. **9.3c-d**, Sally & Richard Greenhill. **9.4a**, Science Photo Library/Professors P.M. Motta & S. Makeabe. **9.4b**, Science Photo Library/Petit Format, Nestle. **9.4c**, Science Photo Library/Alex Bartel. **9.4d**, Sally & Richard Greenhill. **9.6a**, Bruce Coleman. **9.6b**, NHPA/A. Warburton & S. Toon.

The publishers have made every effort to trace copyright holders, but if they have inadvertently overlooked any, they will be pleased to make the necessary arrangements at the first opportunity.